CO-PARENTING WITH A NARCISSIST

COMPLETE GUIDE TO DIVORCE A NARCISSISTIC EX AND TO
HEAL FROM A TOXIC RELATIONSHIP. HOW TO BE A GOOD
MOTHER WHILE RECOVERING FROM EMOTIONAL ABUSE

Mia Warren

Table of Contents

Introduction

Choosing to divorce is especially difficult when it is unclear whether divorcing will improve the lives of your children or make their lives less happy or less safe. Many parents base their decisions about divorce on the best interests of their children, but it is not always evident which path will better serve the children's needs. Staying together in an unhappy marriage may mean that children grow up in an unhappy family. This could affect how children learn to view relationships, which could have a negative impact on their own future partnering. However, if parents who stay together in these marriages do a good job of insulating the children from their conflict and treat one another with respect, the children may end up relatively unscathed. For some families, on the other hand, divorce is the best option for the well-being of the children.

The need to develop a working co-parenting relationship is another crucial task faced by parents. Joint parenting has challenged even for intact families, as we each have preferences for how our children should be raised and our own priorities for how to spend time and money. During and after divorce, these challenges increase. There are logistical issues to consider, such as the need to exchange the children and some of their belongings back and forth from one parent to the other, often several times per week. There is also the need to communicate about decisions that must be made about the children, even though the parents may have a hard time speaking to each other civilly about anything.

One of the biggest pitfalls for families of divorce is parental conflict. For many families, conflict lessens after the divorce is finalized, but for others, conflict remains a key issue. It may occur because of strong feelings each parent has about the divorce itself, but it may also result from fundamentally different beliefs the parents hold about how to raise their children. If not kept in check, conflict between co-parents is arguably the most damaging aspect of divorce for children.

Now that we have touched on some ways that divorce affects parents, we want to take a close look at how divorce affects children. This information will be useful as you prepare a parenting plan with your co-parent and as you engage in day-to-day parenting and co-parenting after the divorce.

The decision to divorce is complicated when divorce conflicts with a parent's personal values, such as when a parent's religious beliefs prohibit divorce or when a parent feels a moral obligation to stay with a spouse due to that spouse's physical, emotional, or financial needs. Finances become particularly relevant when resources are insufficient to provide for two homes. If one or both parents have limited social support, this too may influence the ultimate decision about divorce.

If a couple decides that a separation would be appropriate and safety issues are not a concern, the separation should occur only after a plan is in place for how the parents will share time with the children and how other matters affecting the family will be handled. During the separation, both parents are still parents, and coordination of co-parenting is critical. Good co-parenting is necessary to help the children cope with such a major change in the family. How the parents handle this period is a good measure of how they will handle these issues in the future. Successful co-parenting during separation affirms for parents that they will be able to work as a team on their children's behalf if a divorce does occur.

While the length of the separation depends on the specific circumstances of the family, it is our experience that a period of three to six months is appropriate to achieve the goal of determining if the marriage should continue. A period shorter than three months may not be a sufficient test of what it feels like to live separately, and it is not long enough to expect marriage therapy to resolve the couple's issues. On the other hand, a period greater than six months is rarely necessary. With few exceptions, if parents are unable to decide on the fate of their marriage within six months, it is unlikely that they will gain clarity just by taking a larger amount of time apart. There is also a danger inherent to overextending a separation, as it may lead both spouses to stay stuck in marital limbo.

Chapter 1. Marriage and the Narcissist

Here is a compilation of questions you can ask yourself to determine whether you married a narcissist.

- **Your partner seems to be two different people**

He's the decent guy in public and a cruel, vicious fright at home. Sound acquainted? If it does, you could be living with a narcissist. The narcissist is highly concerned with what people think of him, and he is often a quintessence citizen in public.

At home behind closed doors, he is displeasing, lewd, cruel, or even physically abusive. This can be for any reason - or no reason at all that you can decipher - but most often, when he does not get his way or does not receive the reverence he feels he deserves. He reacts with unbelievable rage when criticized - or when he assumes he was criticized.

- **Your partner attempt to manipulate others against you**

A narcissist lies about you to your friends, family, and even your children. He propagates nasty rumors about you; he tries to share your secrets all in an attempt to turn other people against you. The narcissist perceives you as a rival for attention from these people, and as such, he has to destroy your reputation so that they do not give you any of the love, admiration, or attention he yearns all for himself. He wishes to destroy your good qualities and bring you down to his level.

- **Your partner gaslight you or play mind games**

It's a form of crazy-making created to make the other person feel unsure of reality. It keeps them off-balance and vulnerable to the narcissist's domination. It's a way of controlling the other person and the conversation. Onlya strong person can endure successfully repeated gaslighting. It's an alluring but harmful form of abuse that hinders a person's very perception and reality to the point that they become compliant with whatever the narcissist says. Do not be fooled; he knows very well who is manipulating who.

- **Your partner blames you for everything**

Part of the way narcissism works is to forefend the narcissist from accepting or even seeing when he is to blame. He always upbraids you. It doesn't matter how much he has to writhe things to achieve this; he always accomplishes it. The narcissist wants to mistreat you for things you haven't done because his disorder demands that he punish someone, and he simply cannot stand for it always to be him. The narcissist has a ruthless, sadistic superego that beats him with internal criticisms 24 hours a day. Because of this, he leaps at the chance to take the punishment out on somebody else. It's the only escape from it that he has.

- **Your partner tries to control everything**

Narcissists are grave control freaks. They not only want to control their world, but they also want to control everybody in it. They want to control everything about their partner: their thoughts, feelings, actions, opinions, and everything. Everything the partner does is twisted against them into something terrible. All their motivations are depicted as cruel, manipulative, and abusive. Everything they do hurt or somehow distressed the narcissist unless it is what the narcissist wants them to do.

The weak narcissist uses all of these methods, but he also may attempt to control things through the facade of neediness, clinginess, and insecurity.

"I need to know where you are at all times. I'm too worried if I don't know."

These statements look like neediness, but they are not. They are manipulations to control the other person and dispel their needs as unimportant when compared to the narcissist's needs.

- **Your partner believes everything revolves around him**

Narcissists are completely inconsiderate people. They are selfish to the point of almost appearing inhuman. The narcissist can offer no sympathy, and no shoulder to cry on. Any attempts or effort made to force them to talk about your problems results in either the narcissist "trumping" your issues with their own and making the chinwag all about them or with allegations that you only talk/care about yourself.

Narcissists do not appreciate your feelings as actual feelings; they can only see their partner's feelings as existing simply to affect them. It's like the entire world is a movie, and he is the star.

- **Your partner feels he is qualified for whatever he wants**

Narcissists believe they should have whatever they want, regardless of whether they deserve it or not. They want absolute love, admiration, respect, and it doesn't matter that they are unable to give these things to other people. They want them all and, quite frankly, for their every wish, want, desire and whim to be granted; instantly. The narcissist believes you should provide anything he desires. If you do not do so or attempt to create equality in the relationship, he will portray you as being neglectful, abusive, and uncaring if the narcissist cannot have more than others. He is not interested in inequality at all. Not for himself and not for others.

- **Your partner seems actually to like hurting you and ruining things for you**

This is another distinguishing characteristic of a narcissist. He enjoys hurting others, and he enjoys destroying things that other people care about. Sometimes you can see it in his face when he's done or said something especially cruel to you. He will say or do the worst thing he can come up with and then stand there drinking your reaction in like wine.

Dealing with the Narcissist

Now that you've realized that there is a narcissist in your life, what should you do?

- **Analyze the situation**

Determine how bad the situation is. Try to understand the narcissist's background and the degree of his narcissism. Note or recall what drives him to narcissistic rage. Recall how he tries to punish you. Be aware of the tactics that he uses. Do all these objectively. Being carried away by emotions, shouting or crying will only feed the narcissist.

- **Accept that the narcissist will not change**

Hoping that you will be able to knock some sense into the narcissist or that you could explain and things to enlighten him will not work. As far as the narcissist is concerned, he has done no wrong.

- **Seek help**

Find people – friends, counselors, religious leaders, or parents anyone you can confide in and give advice and emotional support. They can also provide feedback from a neutral viewpoint.

- **Set boundaries**

Write down which boundaries the narcissist cannot trespass and a consequence if they do. Writing things down before talking to the narcissist will help you speak without sounding emotional.

- **Be realistic**

Know the narcissist's limitations and work within those limits. It will only be emotionally draining and a waste of time to expect more from the narcissist than capable. Do not expect him to learn to care because he can't.

- **Remember that your value as a person does not depend on the narcissist**

Don't punish yourself for getting into a relationship with him. Instead, focus on rebuilding your self-esteem, meeting your own needs, and pursuing your interests.

- **Speak to them in a way that will make them aware of how they will benefit**

Instead of voicing your needs, pleading, crying, or yelling; learn to rephrase your statements by emphasizing what the narcissist will gain from it. You have learned to appeal to their selfishness. This is a good way to survive in situations when you cannot leave.

Bring up your ideas to the narcissistic boss when there are witnesses. Having others around to hear your idea will make it difficult to claim credit for it.

- **Find proof of or document any kind of abuse**

Make use of technology, CCTV or video recordings, for example- to document instances of abuse. Find witnesses to back you up.

- **Do not fall for the narcissist's tactics again**

Refresh yourself on his tactics and be on your guard against falling for them again. The narcissist may try to use pity, projection, or hovering. This time, be wiser. It may take practice, as you may have become used to being the "Echo" or codependent. Being aware will help you to resist.

- **Leave**

The best way to deal with the narcissist is not to. For the sake of your emotional and physical well-being, not to mention your sanity, it would be best to leave. If you do leave, expect various tactics from the narcissist to either make your life miserable or to get you back. You will also undergo a period of distress, akin to mourning when you leave.

Seek help and support to get through this stage. Do not be hard on yourself for having allowed yourself to be deceived by the narcissist. Your experience will make you stronger, wiser, and, in time, ready for a healthy relationship. In the meantime, focus on your interests and rebuilding your self-esteem.

Chapter 2. Divorcing a Narcissist

No divorce in the world is easy. However, divorcing a narcissist can be a terrifying time. You may be worried about the safety and well-being of not only yourself but also your children if you have decided to divorce your narcissistic spouse. We will look at the process of divorce and what you should expect. You will need to find help and create a good defense. We will also teach you how to deal with a narcissist in court as it is not as cut and dry as other divorce situations.

After realizing that they are married to a narcissist, many find that the best thing they can do for their overall safety and well-being is to divorce them. It is the best decision for themselves as well as their children. Making the decision may be difficult, but at the end of the day, it will be for you and for your children. It takes bravery and knowledge to venture down the road of divorcing a narcissist.

There are a variety of stressors that surround a "normal" divorce. People worry about the financial aspect and the difficulty and pain it causes to everyone involved. Many couples won't ever have to go to court, and they will be able to work it out through mediation and other techniques. When dealing with a divorce from a narcissist, things are not only more complicated, and you can almost guarantee a judge will end up being involved.

Divorcing a narcissist can become a real mess. People usually work together to stay out of court and find alternatives to the messy process that divorce can entail. When dealing with a narcissist, they will do their best to make things as messy as possible.

While no one wins in a divorce, the narcissist will strive to feel as if they have won. More often than not, when handling divorce, people simply hope for things to be split down the middle. This includes assets and responsibilities. The narcissist is not going to see it this way at all. They are excellent at playing the victim and will have no intention of meeting you in the middle. They will not take the route of mediation or negotiation.

Their goal will be to be the one seen as being in the right. The truth of a narcissist is anything but truthful.

The narcissist is also a master game player. They have been doing it their whole life, and if you think a courtroom is going to stop this behavior, you are sadly mistaken. They will likely up their game because they are truly after a win. They love to hold power, and they do this by keeping other people off-balance. Unfortunately, narcissists tend to be charismatic and charming. This can win favor with a judge or other people involved in your divorce. They will do whatever it takes to wear you down or win the support of the ones that are making decisions. This makes them dangerous to deal with, especially when kids are involved.

Narcissists tend to lack empathy. This means that they will not care at all about the damage they are causing their spouse or their children while working through a divorce.

They can only focus on themselves, so the fact that they are hurting those around them doesn't even cross their radar. Narcissists don't mind burning everything around them to the ground to reach their end goal. While most people will try and be courteous in violent situations like divorce, the narcissist will not care.

They will use anything and everything against their soon to be ex, regardless of the ill-effect it may have. They will even use the children involved as pawns or strategy for the win.

Most people find the court to be a stressful place that they would rather avoid. This is untrue for the narcissist. They love power and control, and they can find a sense of it while dragging you through a difficult and lengthy court process. They find a thrill in the whole process. A narcissist will not have any care as to how long the process of court proceedings take. They may even do their best to prolong the experience, so they can maintain power and control over you. This makes the stress of divorce even worse. It can wear you down, but you must stay strong and persevere. They will do everything they can to keep their grip on you and tear you apart. Rely on your friends, family, and lawyer to keep you strong, and you work through the longer than usual process of divorcing a narcissist.

The narcissist wants you to throw your hands up in the air and say, "I give up." It not only gives them the win but also enables them to feel good about besting you.

They will use this to their advantage with their "friends" and other people to try and continue to make you look bad and to make them look like the victim. Stay strong. You will likely end up in court when divorcing a narcissist as they will refuse to discuss reasonable terms.

One of the reasons that the narcissist prefers court is it helps them avoid accountability. When a judge makes a decision, the narcissist is more comfortable as they don't have any responsibility for how things turn out. Narcissists don't want to be accountable, so whether they win or lose, the court system can be to blame rather than them.

Dealing with a Narcissist in Court

Some narcissists really do have zero empathy and enjoy inflicting severe chaos and intended suffering on others. If you find yourself needing to take your ex to court, therefore, it is wise to become knowledgeable about how to do so.

Let's briefly explore why you would need to beat or expose a narcissist in the court system.

- Financial manipulation, theft, or monetary losses as the result of their narcissism

- Family and domestic disputes with children involved

- Question of resources, assets, shared business or joint ventures

- In extreme cases, physical abuse as devolution of their mental, emotional and psychological abuse inflicted

- Any consequence of their 'evil' and cruel nature

Remember, malignant narcissists can be truly heartless.

What you should know: They've found your wound. They have infected it with negativity. Your wounds are what feeds them, so find healing and put boundaries up. Focus on yourself and not them. This enables you to stay connected to your story and not dragged into theirs.

Deflect

Deflect their 'evil' (unbelievably sadistic and harmful) intentions. Don't allow them to get into your boundaries. Be wise and take preventative measures for your protection. Engaging in some meditative or mindful activity leading up to court can help with this.

Don't expect them to play fair

Assume the worst-case scenarios. Put yourself in their shoes and see all perspectives. How would the worst person in the world word things and try and play it? What angles do they have on you? You may be kind, decent, and a lovely human being, but the narcissist will pick the tiniest negative and amplify it for their gain (and your destruction). Be in the know and wise.

Recognize their arrogance and misplaced confidence

Remember, the narcissist is feeding and playing off some distorted truths and out of place perspectives. Their reality is made from these distortions and elements which can potentially destroy you and your world. Recognizing that a lot of what they say, perceive, and attempt stems from some delusion, illusion, or false belief that can help you overcome the effects effectively and efficiently.

Do not try to expose them as a narcissist

This is vital and crucial to your success. Trying to expose them or label them just looks like 'finger-pointing.' Instead, be humble and actively practice humility, staying centered in your reality and truth. Trying to expose them in a negative light is essentially attracting negativity to you where awareness goes, energy flows.

People will be susceptible to kindness and seeing the positive

Respect is given to those who respect others and choose to act with kindness, not engaging in negative talk. Being sophisticated, courteous, and completely truthful in your words and dealings ultimately makes you appear as the best version of yourself, and naturally exposes the narcissist.

Adopt the principle: "respond, don't react."

Allow him or her to lie and remain calm yourself. Maintaining calm even when the narcissist is blatantly lying or speaking badly about you, trying to represent you in a false light, is the best and most powerful way to get your message across. The words and actions of a narcissist are never on the same page- allow it to play out. Allow them to speak untrue. Focus on the facts and actions, as real actions speak louder than any mistruths or manipulations. In other words, do not resist or react to your partner's story and intended mistruths, as the facts will come to light.

Put the abuse, neglect, and manipulations in the spotlight, not the fact that he is a narcissist

Again, facts are essential, and as much as an emotionally loving and compassionate- insightful society and court system would be ideal, the emotional layers and undertones are overlooked. Do not explain narcissism in any way. The style of manipulating truth from the narcissist can be so effective that it is more significant than truth itself.

There is great power in silence

Silence provides space for truth and hidden things to come to light. Regardless of what is being said against you, the most useful thing you could do for yourself is to be silent simply. All of your partner's darkness, shadow, lies, and buried anger will come powerfully to the forefront. Quite simply, the narcissist cannot stay silent amid truth. They get worked up into violence and self- rage as a result of their lies and manipulations being exposed. The calmer you are, the more they will fall apart. This cannot be stressed enough.

Chapter 3. Child Development and Adapting to Parental Separation

Parenting one size doesn't fit all. The same is valid for talking with your children about the divorce. Every child is at a different developmental stage that requires you to adapt what you say to meet individual levels of maturity and understanding. In every developmental stage, these constants apply:

- Shield children from parental hostility and conflict.

- Give frequent reassurances of your love.

- Create and follow a predictable parenting plan.

- Remain engaged in parenting.

Older Toddlers: 18 Months to 3 Years

If you have a toddler, you are undoubtedly quite familiar with their strong need to be independent. They test limits and begin to express opinions. A primary developmental task for toddlers is to learn to be a unique and separate individual. Temper tantrums and loudly expressed "No!" makeup what some people have termed "the terrible twos." From a developmental standpoint, a lot is going on at this stage. It is sometimes difficult for parents to discern whether the uproar is related to the divorce or is developmentally normal. Signs of distress may include acting sad or lonely, changes in eating or sleeping habits, fears of once-familiar activities or things, and regression to behaviors from an earlier stage of development such as thumb sucking, baby talk, fear of sleeping alone, asking for a bottle, or wanting to wear a diaper again.

As with infants, providing a consistent, predictable routine where their needs are met will help your toddler adjust to the many changes divorce brings. Your toddler will need frequent reassurance of your love through your actions as well as your words. A parenting schedule where they regularly spend time with each of you is optimal. Toddlers do best going no more than three to five days without seeing one parent.

What to Do

Toddlers don't have a good concept of time, so helping them know when they will be at each house will ease transition jitters. Make a calendar where they can see it and use stickers or colored pens to designate "Mom time" and "Dad time." Help them count the number of sleep. For example, "You have three nights of sleep with Mommy, and then you go to Dad's house. Let's count them together, one, two and three Daddy." The more light-heartedand matter-of-fact your tone, the better for your toddler.

Children love books about themselves. Make a small book with photographs of familiar items and routines at each parent's house and read it together before changing homes. I've known children to carry these books until the paper is nearly worn through. Check your library or bookstore for age-appropriate books about divorce.

What to Say

Toddlers need a short and simple explanation about the divorce. You will likely be asked to repeat it many times as they work to understand what it means.

Preschoolers: 3 to 5 Years

Preschoolers experience a huge boost in cognitive and physical abilities. They are more self-sufficient than before and can carry out basic self-care tasks like dressing themselves, brushing their teeth, and going to the bathroom unassisted. Their vocabulary has increased, allowing them to understand better and express feelings and ideas. Preschoolers can be big talkers! Even with this growth in cognitive ability, there are still areas of confusion. For example, if they overhear parents discussing or arguing about parenting time, they are very likely to make an inaccurate conclusion that they are responsible for the divorce.

Preschoolers benefit from routine and a predictable schedule. They can feel overwhelmed by the multiple changes that accompany divorce. They are sometimes afraid a parent will abandon them.

Preschoolers may show signs of distress like clinginess or fear of exploring the world, regressing to earlier developmental stages, feeling responsible for the divorce or a parent's feelings, acting sad, showing uncharacteristic outbursts of anger, and trying to control their environment.

What to Do

As you talk with your preschooler about the divorce, assure him of your love and abiding presence in his life. Breathe calmly, smile, and relax as you describe what's going to happen. Gently touch a hand or rub your child's back as you talk.

What to Say

Reassurance is the name of the game with preschoolers. Tell them what's going to happen without turning it into a crisis.

Early School Agers: 6 to 8 Years

School-age children are becoming quite savvy about the world. Their cognitive abilities are growing by leaps and bounds, giving them a much broader understanding of feelings and the ability to regulate them better. Family relationships are important and provide a strong base from which to venture into the world of school and friends. When the divorce disrupts this secure base, it can affect the normal developmental milestone of moving away from the family as the primary source of social interactions.

Children at this age are well aware of rules and become very disappointed when they believe a parent isn't following rules. They deeply miss the parent they are not with and sometimes side with one parent against the other.

Signs of distress include major changes in grades or attitudes about school, an increase in physical symptoms like headaches and stomachaches, exaggerated emotions like moping, crying, acting sad or lonely, and a general lack of enthusiasm.

What to Do

Provide a loving environment for your children. Maintain a predictable routine with clearly communicated expectations for behavior. Be a good listener, accepting all feelings while you help your children attach words to the feelings they share. Keep your children away from any conflict you may have with the other parent. Be that secure base they need as they go out and explore.

What to Say

At this age, your children are going to want some details. They've probably noticed the conflict and maybe anticipating your news about the divorce. Even so, they will need a gentle explanation and reassurance of your love.

Preteens: 9 to 12 Years

In this developmental stage, children become even more independent, and friends play an important role in their lives. Preteens are much more aware of what other people think, especially their peers. They might feel ashamed or embarrassed about the divorce, sometimes to the point of keeping quiet about it. They are selfishly and appropriately focused on their own lives, and they don't like it when they see the divorce messing things up for them.

Preteens have made huge leaps in cognitive ability and are better able to understand the nuances of the problems parents are having. They are likely to feel torn between parents, and they worry when they believe a parent isn't okay. Conflicts tend to occur when they don't get something they want. They are usually very good at pushing guilt buttons, blaming parents, and the divorce when things don't go as they'd like.

Signs of distress about the divorce show up in increased physical symptoms like headaches, stomachaches, or general "just not feeling well"; a dramatic change in grades or attitudes about school; fighting with peers or siblings; acting like the divorce is no big deal and premature sexual activity.

What to Do

Your preteen will vigilantly watch how you handle things and will be reasonably quick to judge your actions. Parents need to model good self-care and healthy ways to express emotions. Preteens need to involve and alert parents to help them with the increasingly complex issues they face in the world. They will want to know what's going on and will push for details. Be cautious about how much you share. They can handle more information than younger children, but they must be protected from the specifics of adult problems.

What to Say

Your preteens will hold you accountable for your actions, sometimes brutally so. When you talk with them about the divorce, it's essential to keep it real and be honest without sharing too much.

Adolescents: 13 to 19 Years

The primary developmental task for adolescents is to get ready to leave home and live in the adult world. Yet they aren't entirely as prepared as they may think. There are developmental milestones to achieve. They still don't have a realistic view of the future, and they lack real-world experience. They have their version of "magical thinking" where they believe bad things could never happen to them. Part of their parents' job is to compassionately help them learn responsibility for their actions as they gain experience to leave the nest successfully.

Like preteens, adolescents are focused on themselves. They resent the divorce when it disrupts their lives. Because of divorce, they may have greater responsibilities at home, less money, and overworked and unavailable parents. Teens' cognitive ability has increased to make them appear to think like adults, although they aren't quite there yet. They are good at figuring out what's going on with their parents and will endlessly push for details. Be cautious about sharing too much because it isn't in their best interest.

Teensthat are getting ready to leave home feel anxious about this huge step and will need compassionate parents mentally and physically be available as they work through the fear and excitement. Teens may feel some responsibility for the breakup because of things they did or did not do. It's important to reassure them the divorce in no way is their fault.

Signs of distress include premature sexual activity, excessive drug or alcohol use, problems in the school including truancy or suspension, negative attitude, criticisms of parents, leaving home prematurely, or showing reluctance ever to leave, canceling plans for college, and moving out.

What to Do

Maintain stability in your teen's living arrangements with a few life changes as possible. Teens need reasonable limits with clearly articulated expectations and consequences. Parents must stay attentive and keep on top of monitoring daily activities. There is a great need for excellent communication between parents around issues like rules, curfews, homework, cell phones and Internet use, and cars.

What to Say

Teens will be very interested in the logistics of your divorce and will do best when they have a say in the schedule. They want to know you are taking their needs into account. If possible, reassure them that their activities and interactions with friends won't change. They need to be told they aren't responsible for the divorce. Because their social lives are busy, teens do best with plenty of warning before changes occur in the family schedule. Offer multiple times to talk about what will happen and then compassionately answer their questions. The sample script for preteens also works for adolescents.

Chapter 4. Guidelines for Answering Children's Questions about Divorce

The following questions are among some of the toughest children will ask when parents' divorce or separate. In some cases, there is a straight-forward answer, while for others it may not be easy to give kids an adequate or full explanation. This is often due to not knowing what to expect next and realizing that there can be several solutions or outcomes on the horizon, without knowing which one is going to prevail. In general, it's best to keep your response brief and to the point, and let your kids ask more questions. Make sure they understand that you are working for the best outcome possible.

Is this my fault? What did I do wrong to make mommy/daddy leave?

Firstly, assure them that they are not to blame for the divorce and that they did nothing wrong to make the separation or divorce happen. Furthermore, it's essential to explain that there is nothing they could do to make their parents split and that they are the reason that both parents will stay in touch and make sure everything stays as normal as possible.

Why don't you love daddy/mommy anymore?

This is a tough question that can garner several responses, depending on the specific circumstances. Many parents who separate continue to care or show respect for one another, where the split is amicable and civil. When separating from a narcissistic parent, it can be quite the opposite, and cause a lot of grief for the other parent. To the child or children, any love between the parents can be lost, making them sad and upset. They will ask why you (or your ex) no longer have these feelings, and they may fear that your love for them will be lost in the same way. Don't be afraid to be candid, in cases where the spouse is narcissistic or abusive. This might be an essential way to communicate with the kids when you find yourself in an emergency move-out scenario, or need to explain things without worrying the kids too much, though making sure they understand that their needs come first:

- The reason we left your mommy/daddy is that they hurt us. We still love them, but until they can change and stop hurting us, we have to live in different homes.

- I know it's not easy to be away from mommy/daddy, but they can hurt you or me. This is because they are sick and need help. I hope they can get help and change, so we can live as a family again.

- We both love you very much, no matter what happens between us, and we will work together to see you and make your life the best.

- Sometimes, parents can't live together anymore, but they both care for the kids. This love will never end because you are our children, and we love you more than anyone.

Allow them to get used to make each day, week, and month at a time and focus on other aspects of their lives that are important, such as school, homework, seeing their friends, and other families. Keep them occupied with as many constructive ideas and projects as possible, to keep their minds focused on better times ahead.

Whose side should I be?

Children should always be reassured that they do not have to take sides. If the other parent tries to sway them or feel the pressure to do so, let them know that you love them regardless of how they feel during this difficult time. They don't have to agree or disagree with either parent, but simply get along with them and make the best of the situation. It may help to use some of the following statements:

"You don't have to take sides. We both love you, and our separation is not your fault."

"Don't worry about taking one side. You don't have to agree with either your mom or dad. We both love you."

The situation becomes more complicated with a narcissistic ex-spouse, who will manipulate the children into taking their side over yours and convince them that you are the blame for the separation. Unfortunately, even in cases where an ex is abusive and hurtful towards the kids, they may take his/her side out of fear of retaliation and want to avoid any conflict that may occur between them and the abusive parent. A narcissist is a good manipulator, and they will use this cruel tactic on their kids to get their way and control them. When this occurs, know that your children may cause you to feel hurt or rejection as a result of siding with your ex. They may feel guilty about it already and calling them out on it only worsens the situation. Instead, consider handling it with the following statements:

"I know you are angry with me right now, and you think that your mother/father is right. Please know that I still love you, regardless of how you feel."

"It's up to you to decide how you feel. I still love you regardless of this."

"I will not tell you which side to take, because it's not fair, because I love you."

It's also important to express your feelings and gauge your children's sense of empathy towards you. It's good to know if they understand that you will continue to love and care for them, even if they decide to live with your ex-spouse on their own (when they are old enough to do so).

"When you take sides, it hurts me a lot because I value how you feel about me and your mother/father."

"You don't have to agree with me, but I would like to stay in touch because I care about you."

Expressing your emotions is imperative to keeping the connection healthy and strong between you and your children. Let them know that regardless of your ex's comments or attempts to sway them away from you, they will always be loved and treated with respect. This will not always be when they spend time with the other parent, and unfortunately, they will learn the narcissist parent's traits the hard way, by firsthand experience.

Children of narcissistic parents will always be made to feel as though they can do better. This may begin in small doses at first, where the parent asserts that they love your child as much as you do. Still, they will systematically break down different aspects of their personality traits, making them feel inadequate so that they can feel superior over them.

Learning about these scenarios may give your children insight on how to handle possibly difficult situations by discussing some of these possibilities with them today. Consider some past experiences you had with the other parent, and give your kids a "heads up" without demonizing the other parent or using the opportunity to "attack" or invalidate your ex's parental role, even where it may seem accurate. Always talk to your kids in a way that is proactive and reasonable and give them an indication of what to expect from the other parent.

They may be a perfectionist and have high expectations that simply do not end. Assure the kids that this is not their concern, and not to worry if they are not perfect or adequately fulfill their role within the narcissist's parents mind.

Let your kids know that their talent and abilities in life will be measured, judged and assessed by many people, which may give some good advice, some bad, as well as a mix of good and bad reviews. Compare the ex-spouse to being a different "judge" each time, and that there is no absolute way to please some people, it's important to follow their dreams and not let anyone else get in the way of your goals.

Why does mommy/daddy get angry? Is there anything I can do to fix this?

It's difficult to see children struggle as a result of emotional distress caused by one parent onto the other or the children. Kids are good listeners and understand a great deal from a young age. For this reason, it becomes essential for them to know that when one parent is angry, even when they blame the kids for the split, it's important not to internalize their anger, and keep a safe distance.

Mommy/daddy wants me to live with them, should I?

This is a difficult question that is planted onto the children by your ex. They will try to make the kids feel responsible for where they live, even if the court determines they are the best living with you. You may be tempted to ask your children who they want to live with, especially if they have a say and old enough to decide. They may be hesitant because they don't want to disappoint you if they choose to move in with your ex, or want to remain where they are (with you) and feel as if they're deceiving the other parent by not living with them instead.

This is a difficult decision placed on them, and while there is no easy way to navigate around it, you can assure them that you support their decision either way, provided they are well taken care of and safe. If moving in with your ex-spouse causes conflict between them and your children, reassure them, they can always return to you, if life becomes difficult and unbearable with the other parent.

There are many difficult and challenging questions children will pose, at all ages, when parents split. There will never be an easy way to deal with all of them, which means communication, and expressing your love for them becomes paramount. Even where kids may blame you, or become angry with you about the divorce, it's important to remind them that you love them regardless. This is an unconditional love that they will never receive from their other, narcissistic parent.

Chapter 5. Parental Alienation

Co-parenting is never easy, but with narcissists, it is entirely different. When relationships fail without children, the dissolution is usually relatively quick and permanent, but when children are involved, that relationship can never be fully dissolved. You can never fully disentangle yourself from your ex-partner if you have children with him or her, and because of that, even if you divorce or leave a narcissist, you may be forced to continue some degree of contact.

You must be prepared to deal with the narcissist playing mind games with his children, as well. When in a conflict, he may stop giving any attention or affection to them, and he will always push the blame on you to make you look worse in your children's eyes. He will say that you said he could not do something, or that you made him so angry that he could not take them to the amusement park as he had promised. This tactic, known as parental alienation, is meant to drive a wedge between you and your children to hurt you.

It occurs when one parent deliberately or unconsciously turns a child or children against another parent. This process typically happens during a custody battle. How does the alienating parent operate?

Some common tactics include:

- Badmouthing the other parent or within the child's hearing

- Ignoring or undermining timesharing/visitation orders, so the child doesn't see or talk to the other parent much;

- Withdrawing emotionally from the child if he or she shows affection for the other parent;

- Telling the child he or she must choose between the two parents;

- Making the child believe the other parent is a danger or threat using verbal persuasion and sometimes engaging in more extravagant activities, such as faking bruises to pretend to have been beaten, soliciting other trusted adults to ratify made-up stories or even employing drugs or alcohol to make the child more persuadable

- Making fun of the other parent's family and friends, and keeping the child's contact with them to a minimum or avoiding contact with them entirely.

- Such actions can turn even a loving, empathetic child against a parent.

The child can react in many ways to these attempts. He or she can resist the persuasion, turn against the targeted parent to avoid losing the affection of the caregiving parent or come to believe in the inherent "badness" of the targeted parent and start inventing reasons to validate this perception.

The psychological turmoil created by the alienating behavior unsurprisingly can damage the parent-child relationships.

Unwinding the harm done is not often straightforward. Studies suggest that the damage is harder to reverse the longer the alienation is allowed to continue.

The narcissist knows that his image and reputation are dependent upon his children having respect for and looking up to him. The narcissist has to look good as compared to everyone else, especially in the eyes of his children. He must constantly condition them to respect him and to look up to him.

The narcissist must show his children that he is better than everyone else to keep their respect for him. He needs their undying loyalty, or they will not subscribe to his causes and his beliefs. To get this, he must talk bad about everyone else around him. This includes talking bad about the other parent.

The child initially grows confused about the narcissist talking bad about the other parent. The child grows to hate the side of him or herself that is like a parent that they see as weak. They try to suppress anything inside themselves that reminds them of their other parent. They try to reject both themselves and the 'weak' parent.

The narcissistic parent and child learn how to badmouth and gossip behind the other parent's back. The narcissist constantly lets the child have 'secrets'. They encourage the child to hide things from the other parent and to get away with things. The narcissist encourages the child to be dishonest and deceptive in their relations with the other parent. What mommy or daddy doesn't know won't hurt him.

The narcissist plays favorites and makes the child think he or she is in on something 'special' by hiding things and sneaking around. They resist any guidance that the non-narcissistic parent has that would allow the child to grow into a healthy adult.

Children who reject their non-narcissistic parent are in for a cruel and unexpected surprise, however. The proud child who rejected all responsibility and manners during their childhood will realize that other people in the working world don't enjoy their proud and arrogant attitude. They don't fit in. Their romantic partners leave them when they discover their bad temperament and proud attitude.

The proud and arrogant child grows up into a disgruntled adult who thinks the world isn't fair. They are chronically grumpy and unhappy that they are never able to make things go the way they want them to. They throw adult-sized tantrums that wind them up in jail or prison. They ruin their relationships with their immaturity and adult-sized tantrums. They tell their boss off and get fired. The narcissist loves that the narcissistic child must keep moving back home. This makes the narcissist feel needed and useful; to cause codependency in his child. He doesn't want the child to grow and mature and leave the nest; he wants the child to be his play friend long into adulthood.

Their attitude toward others means they can only partner up with an equally broken and contentious person. Thus the narcissist ends up in a relationship with someone else who is just as reactive as they are. Thus, the fighting and power struggle to ensure in the relationship and the romantic relationships they are in the lead to divorces of epic proportions.

The non-narcissistic parent cannot stoop to the level of the narcissist and badmouth the narcissist once he has already badmouthed them. Then, the child is already loyal to the narcissist.

The child will go back to the narcissist and 'tattle' on what the non-narcissistic parent said about him or her. Or, the parental alienation syndrome child will learn to hate the non-narcissistic parent, being brainwashed by the narcissist into believing that the non-narcissistic parent is picking on the narcissist.

The narcissistic child will pit both parents against one another so that both parents will try to one-up each other constantly and for the remainder of both their natural lives. The narcissistic child, who learns to play this game, in the end, causes both parents to spoil them with money, trips and objects.

The non-narcissistic parent can tell the child that they don't participate or encourage gossip or drama. If they consistently say this over and over, the child will learn that he or she has the right to assert his or her boundaries when others are trying to commiserate with them or air their dirty adult laundry to the child. Their growth will be stunted in constantly getting caught up in other people's drama. A non-narcissistic parent can teach the child to be concerned about their personal growth above all else.

Contributing Factors to Parental Alienation

There aren't many valid reasons why a parent should alienate their children from the other parent. But, there may be factors that are causing your ex to have some faulty thinking. It doesn't make it right, but understanding your ex's thinking can help you understand what's happening, and how to combat the effects on your children.

Legal Battles

Sometimes parents are unable to reach any kind of agreement on how access to the children should be divided. The court is usually the only way forward, but legal battles in themselves can create an adversarial tone to the parenting relationship. The resident parent can feel attacked or that you and the court are questioning their parenting. They can also feel that the court isn't listening to them, or that they're being treated unfairly through the process.

Child Maintenance

The resident parent can feel that there isn't enough money being paid as maintenance. Often, it doesn't matter how much money is being paid, and it will never feel like enough. Sometimes, the resident parent can confuse child maintenance with spousal maintenance. Essentially, they want to continue living in the manner they did while in a relationship with you, but obviously, financial priorities change when you have children.

Emotional Hurt

The alienating parent may feel that you have rejected them, or otherwise emotionally hurt them. They may feel that you are responsible for their feelings and alienate you as a punishment. They can also assume that the children feel the same way they do, even if this isn't true.

Insecurity

Sometimes an alienating parent can feel insecure about their relationship with their child. If they believe that you have a strong bond with the child, it makes them question and thinks that it will impact their parent-child relationship.

Family Instability

If the alienating parent has low-income family relationships with their own family, they sometimes feel the need to keep their children close to them. They don't want the children to have the same relationship with them as they have with their family, but may not realize that in doing this, they're cutting them off from you and your family.

New Partner

Sometimes an alienating parent may try to replace you as the biological parent with their new partner. The new partner is presented to the children as being incredible, and the children may be encouraged to call the new partner 'Dad' or 'Mum'.

Emotional Instability

Sometimes the alienating parent has some form of emotional instability. Their own emotional needs become the priority, and they can cut all kinds of contact between you and your children. They want to control your contact and access, but they may also want to control what happens during your communication.

History

You may have noticed that your ex didn't like it when you or the children had an opinion that was different from their own. They may have tried to convince you, and the children that they were right all along. If you noticed this behavior during your relationship, it's unlikely to change after you've separated.

Age ofthe Children

The age of the children can be a contributing factor. It's much easier for younger children to take what either parent says as gospel. Young kids simply expect parents not to lie to them, present half-truths, or even to have a different perspective than they do. As well as that, young kids don't have the same well of memories to draw on, and the alienating parent's opinions may taint all their memories of you and versions of events. Older children can be more open to questioning the alienating parent. They also have more independent memories of you that haven't been influenced by the alienating parent.

Chapter 6. Narcissistic Manipulative Tactics

Narcissists have a burning desire to be appreciated at all costs. In their minds, they are all that matters. Everyone and everything else is subordinate to their needs when it comes to gratification. While most people believe they are aware of everything that goes on around them and is in full control, it is not always easy to deal with narcissists. Narcissists have perfected the art of manipulation.

Narcissists are exploitative, dishonest and barely show empathy. By learning about the techniques they use, you can take the first step towards learning how to loosen their manipulative grip on you and restore your life.

The following are some of the techniques that narcissists use to pin you down:

- **Gaslighting**

Gaslighting is a form of psychological manipulation where the victim is manipulated into doubting their sanity, feelings or instinct (Stark, 2019). Victims end up wondering whether their version of reality is the truth or if it is distorted. Gaslighting breeds self-doubt to a point where you cannot trust yourself to think straight. You no longer feel you have a right to call out the abuser for mistreating you.

Common examples of gaslighting statements include the following phrases:

"A lot of people have been saying you are..."

"It's nothing, and you are just jealous."

"That's not how it happened, are you sure?"

Gaslighting disrupts your cognitive function, and most victims develop cognitive dissonance. You end up with two extreme beliefs about the same thing. You find yourself stuck in a position where you don't trust yourself enough to believe in what you know is right, or whether you should trust what your abuser has made you believe the truth.

- **Projection**

Narcissists will never see their flaws as a representation of who they are. Instead, they look for someone to hold accountable. Projection is a defense strategy which helps them make someone else responsible for their negative attributes. Instead of taking responsibility for their actions, they hold someone else in contempt.

Projection is not a trait that only narcissists experience everyone does it at some point. However, while ordinary people's projection might be subtle, a narcissist's projection can be abusive psychologically and at times, physically.

Narcissists have deeply rooted toxicity and shame that they cannot own up. Instead, they project it on someone else, who ends up feeling guilty and ashamed (Metzl, 2009). In a relationship with a needy partner, instead of admitting their neediness, they can project it on you and say you are a clingy partner. This way, they don't have to deal with their problems.

Projection is essentially about shifting blame. They must come out on top all the time. In the unlikely event that things don't turn out their way, they can blame it on you or everyone else. Instead of living a happy and independent life, you are shackled to a fragile ego that you must tread carefully not to hurt.

- **Shaming**

If you get into a disagreement with a narcissist, their easiest clap back is to shame you. Shaming is something that people use all the time, even those who are not narcissists. The difference is that while other people use shaming perhaps to call you out on something wrong, narcissists shame you to trim your power. If they feel you are growing stronger and out of their grip, shame makes you belittle yourself, and get back to the level they think you deserve.

Narcissists are obsessed with their persona. They shame anyone who might be basking in the glory of their wins so your esteem can wither away. They don't do well with other people's pride. Any hint that you are making powerful strides is met with shaming statements, so your self-worth diminishes, and you believe in nothing but their opinion of yourself.

The venue or audience does not hold a narcissist back from shaming you. Whether you are in public or alone together, if they feel the moment is right, a narcissist will shame you by making snide comments that hurt or belittle your presence.

- **Devaluation**

In a real sense, narcissists love to be worshipped. They can cultivate a culture of worship in you without your knowledge. At the beginning of your relationship, a narcissist can put you on a pedestal. In this stage, you idealize them and see nothing but good things about them. You are invested in this new relationship that everything else around you doesn't matter. As this happens, you might also cut off some of your friends because you feel they don't see you in the same light as the narcissist does. They are a burden, a bother or outright jealous that you have something beautiful, someone who adores you.

A typical example is starting a relationship with a narcissist who just broke up with someone. In the beginning, you are the best thing that ever happened in their lives. They trash their exes and tell you how amazing you are, how different you are from everyone else. When they have had their fair share of fun, you get devalued in the same way their former partners were. Upon careful investigation, you might realize the former partner went through the same thing you are going through with their previous partner.

- **Baiting**

Every narcissist needs a platform upon which they can practice their cruelty without reprimand. To do this, they pretend to create a sense of security. Once you are in, you are trapped. One of the techniques they use is baiting. A simple discussion soon turns into an argument which escalates into chaos with someone who seems to have no idea about respect. Initially, you might respond to the subtle argument politely, but the real intention was to wreak havoc.

Narcissists take time to learn about you. They know what your insecurities are, words that trigger your emotions and so forth. They know topics that are dear to you, things in your past that you feel strongly about, which might provoke you. These are the things they target. This is how you are baited.

Once you fall for the trick and hit rock bottom, they take a step back and pretend to care. They ask if you are okay, and insist they had no intention of agitating you. All of this is not true but because you are already worked up, you take the apology and believe their words. This will repeatedly happen until you realize the pattern and notice the malice behind it.

- **Control**

Toxic narcissists and abusers always strive to stay in control. They feel good when things are going according to plan. They must control everyone and everything in their environment.

In a relationship, a narcissist will try to alienate you from your social circles. They will talk about how your family and friends are a bad influence on you, and that you should cut them off. Once you are isolated, and they have you wrapped around their finger, they can do with you as they please. Every aspect of your life is under their control, from your social networks (online and offline) to finances. They must be briefed on everything you do, or you might be banned from engaging anyone else. Some victims have locked away from the rest of the world as a form of punishment.

Narcissists find it very easy to conjure conflicts whenever they feel their victim is enjoying too much freedom. The idea here is to make you lose your balance, feel vulnerable and follow their instructions. This is the reason why they create frivolous arguments about petty issues.

- **Generalizations**

Some narcissists are very lazy at their own game. Instead of carefully studying a situation and determining how to respond amicably, they generalize with a blanket statement that ignores all elements of the discourse. If you have a differing opinion, it is easier for them to relegate your idea into a general label.

Why do narcissists generalize everything? Their concept of generalization is as a result of an insane stereotype and schema about society. They have prevailing assumptions which must align with their expectations. It is almost impossible to rationalize an argument with such a narcissist because they see everything as a subtle attack on their personality.

- **Pushing boundaries**

Narcissists will always push your boundaries to see what you can do and to identify your limits. They try to cross as many of your boundaries as possible without consequences. Each time they do this, their resolve grows stronger. This also explains why survivors of emotional and physical abuse who reconcile with and go back to their abusers usually suffer worse damage than the past incidents.

Narcissists and other abusers pretend to be remorseful. They lure you back with empty promises that they will change. Some might even join a program that should help them change. However, once they have you where they want you, everything changes and your suffering intensifies. In their minds, pushing your limits is the perfect punishment you deserve for standing up against their abuse, and more importantly, for coming back. They believe you came back because the past incidents were not enough. They have to take things a notch higher so you can feel real pain, pain enough for you not to return.

- **Accountability**

One of the tactics narcissists love to use is to change the subject and divert attention to themselves. They do this to escape responsibility. A narcissist must never be held accountable for anything. If such a discussion is going on, it serves their interests well if they divert attention to something else, something that suits them.

In therapy, a victim of narcissistic abuse might mention a period of neglect that hurt them emotionally. Instead of listening, the narcissist will cut in by mentioning a mistake that the victim committed a week ago. Each time you try to hold them accountable, they find a reason to divert attention from that situation by identifying something to blame you for, in an attempt to prove that you deserve what you got.

- **Threats**

Narcissists will create impossible expectations and challenging obstacles in your life so that they can punish you for failing to live up to expectations. Most arguments with narcissists are futile. From the very beginning, you are destined to fail. The fact that you tried will be used against you.

Instead of engaging in a healthy disagreement or argument maturely, narcissists will try to highlight the consequences of failing to comply. Even as you participate in what you think is an honest and mature discourse, at the back of your mind, you cannot ignore the lingering threat.

- **Triangulation**

Triangulation is a common trait in malignant narcissists. They introduce family members, friends, former partners, workmates or even strangers into the picture to make you jealous and create an air of uncertainty around you. Each time they need their perspective validated, they use someone else.

It is one of the best diversionary tactics narcissists use because you end up thinking that if someone else, a stranger to your relationship sees things differently, then probably your perspective is flawed. Your attention moves away from their abuse to a faux belief that they are right, highly sought after and desirable. Instead of addressing your abuse, you question yourself. If someone else agrees with them, then the only sensible option is that you are wrong.

Chapter 7. Tips for Co-Parenting with a Narcissist

What if you end a relationship with a narcissist, but have children together? This complicates the situation, but it isn't hopeless. Your child can still grow up healthy and happy; you will have to be the responsible, consistent figure in their lives

You know what it's like to be the partner of a narcissist, but what about a child? It's important to understand what your kid is going through if their other parent - your ex - is a narcissist. Depending on how long you were with your ex with a child or children in the mix, you've probably noticed the unhealthy aspects of their parenting style.

Just like with their partner, a narcissist won't pay attention to what their child needs or wants. The narcissist's needs always take priority, so the child learns from a young age that what they want doesn't matter. They are never nurtured and taught to feel safe. They feel small and insignificant. These kids may not even know how to express what they want and need because that type of thinking has never been encouraged. Their sense of self can be very stunted.

To counter this messaging, encourage your child to pursue their dreams. Ask them questions about how they feel and what they think about things, whether it's movies, friendships, or the separation from your ex. If your kid expresses a lot of insecurity and self-doubt, gently guide them, so they feel like they have support, but also freedom. This guidance can be applied to finding a hobby or having conversations about what they're feeling about their life.

Narcissists frequently put very high expectations on their kids. They believe their kids reflect on them, so they push them to succeed. The child won't feel loved unless they're doing something well, looking a certain way, or thinking certain things. The narcissist might be very critical, judgmental, and withholding when their kid inevitably "fails." The child will feel like nothing they do is ever good enough. It's very common for these kids to have low self-esteem and very poor self-worth because they believe love is conditional.

Pushing back against the belief that love is conditional is arguably the most important thing you can do as a parent. Parents should always be the people a child can rely on for love, no matter what. If your ex isn't capable of being that, it's more important that you take on that role wholeheartedly. Always celebrate your child, especially when they "fail" or don't meet the expectations your ex set up. Let them know your love isn't dependent on their successes; you love them because of who they are, not what they do. You can still encourage them to improve and set goals, but never attach your attention and affection to an outcome. Be sure to tell them you love them no matter what, too. Words are powerful.

When you get upset, don't lose control around your kid. That includes any strong emotions, like grief or anger. However, you should encourage your kid to express those emotions when they need to. Be a shoulder to cry on and a safe place. When they get angry, help them figure out healthy ways of expression instead of punishing them. They'll see that you are emotionally stable and nurturing, even when their other parent can't be.

If your ex wants to be involved in your children's lives, there are certain things you can do to make the process easier and safer.

Set Communication Boundaries

As a co-parent, you will need to talk to your ex. However, you can decide when you speak and about what. Your ex will always try to push the boundaries and use any opportunity to get under your skin. They may even try to get you so angry that you lose control, which gives them leverage over you. Avoid talking on the phone or in-person if your ex likes to go on rants, emotionally abuse you, or otherwise try to get you worked up. Stick to emails, which give you more control over what you say, and it keeps everything in writing.

It's impossible to control what your ex says when your kid is with them. However, when the kid is with you, you can set more boundaries. Expect your ex to want to talk to the kid a lot. Set a schedule and stick to it. For example, no phone call on school nights later than 8 pm, and only after homework is done. Your ex will probably try to break these rules, so stand your ground. If you believe your ex is using phone calls to emotionally abuse your child or disregard any other agreements made in court, consider recording them. In many places, you must tell your ex their call is being recorded. Talk to a lawyer before moving forward.

If things are too complicated and challenging, get a parent coordinator. Judges appoint these people, and they act as a mediator between you and your ex, so you don't need to talk to them unless necessary. The parent coordinator handles scheduling visits and any other communication.

Protect Your Child

If your co-parent has custody or visitation rights, it's hard to control what your ex says or does. However, you should never use your child as a messenger pigeon. Don't ask them to communicate with your ex on your behalf or ask them to spy. This puts the kid in a very awkward and possibly scary situation. You can find out how they're being treated and what they're doing just by having normal conversations. If you're concerned by something they say, ask them a question like, "How does that make you feel?" It can be hard to know what to say, and there are certain things your child might not want to talk about with you, so getting your kid to counseling is an excellent idea.

Be especially aware of how your child's milestones might affect your ex. As healthy kids get older, they will become more independent. Narcissists typically resist this aspect of child-rearing because they want to keep control.

You will feel a lot of emotions, especially negative ones, during a co-parenting scenario with a narcissist. But don't use your child as a sounding board for your frustrations with your ex. This not only makes the kid feel like they need to comfort you and manage your feelings; it makes them feel torn about their love for their other parent. They might instinctively resist your criticisms and jump to your ex's defense, or become angry and even scared of their other parent. This puts them in your ex's crosshairs while also making mad at you for turning their child against them. The already-fragile co-parenting situation becomes even more volatile and stressful for your child.

The Most Written Detail, the Best

Co-parenting with a narcissist is complicated, and every situation is a little different. The best thing you can do is to keep detailed records. Right at the beginning, when you start seeing a family law attorney, tell them what's going on with your ex. Tell them they are a narcissist and are "high-conflict," which is a legal term for these types of custody scenarios. In your custody agreement, write down every detail, like who pays for what, the days and times they have visitation, holiday visitations, and more.

Having detailed records is also important as life continues because your ex is unlikely to follow the rules peacefully. They will try to push back, and having records of their bad behavior protects you and your children. If they cancel or try to move around visitation, write it down. If they refuse to pay for something or are late with the money, write it down. Using phone calls to manipulate your kid? Let them know you are going to be recording the call. Any communication between you two should be saved, if possible. This evidence lets you hold them accountable.

Take Care of Yourself

Self-care is not selfish. As a parent, this has never been truer. If you let yourself get drained, worn down, and depleted, you'll have nothing to offer your kid. You'll have less patience, less stability, and more irritability. Your kid won't come to you because they'll see how exhausted you are, and they won't want to burden you. Not only will you not have the physical or emotional energy to care for them, but you're modeling unhealthy habits they will imitate. They won't know how to take care of themselves and like you, and they'll burn out. For both your sake and the sake of your kids, practice good self-care.

Find a Community

Your child may fundamentally lack a second parent, but that doesn't mean you're in this alone. Don't burden yourself by believing you are your kid's only adult role model. Find a community that is supportive of both you and your child and rich with healthy, loving people who can encourage your child's emotional growth. A community can also help you by giving your friends to vent to, who are happy to babysit, and more. People need community, especially when life gets rough.

Don't Let Your Ex Manipulate You

To be a good parent, one of the best things you can do is not let your ex infect you with toxic thoughts and beliefs. As you know, they will use your child as a weapon. Expect to hear things like, "How could you do this to our family?" They will try to make you guilty for leaving and say that the separation is bad for your children. When they see you aren't budging, they'll move on to the custody agreement, and say, "That's bad, too." Don't believe it. They will be just as critical and selfish in their relationship with their child as they were with you, so leaving and sticking to a particular arrangement is the only healthy thing to do.

Your ex probably won't stay quiet about their frustrations and will trash you on social media and to anyone who will listen. Having people, even friends, believe you are a bad parent can be hard. Keep standing firm and remember that this is what's best for your child. The people who know you will be supportive.

Chapter 8. Helping Your Children Through a Divorce

The way that you communicate with your child can make or break your relationship. From the smallest non-verbal child to an adult, people want to feel heard, understood, and accepted by their parents. This is particularly important when a child feels insecure or threatened, as he will during or after a divorce. Your child is undergoing what is probably the most significant stressor in his life to date and may not feel that he is your priority anymore. Your communication methods set the stage for your child to view your divorce as a sad event rather than the cataclysm that destroyed life as she knew it.

The parent-child relationship provides the basic foundation for a child to learn how to interact with others, such as peers, and later, in adult intimate relationships. Thankfully, there are simple skills you can learn that will help you communicate more healthily with your child. These specific, teachable communication methods can help your child to learn about, process, and accept his feelings, while also feeling strong enough to change how he responds to his feelings. You can use these skills with children of all ages, during even the most heated encounters. All of these techniques help show your child that you love him, and will defuse tension and anger so that you can truly hear what your child wants to tell you. The basic communication techniques that we will cover are mirroring, curiosity, empathy, and validation. It is also essential to take responsibility for your own words and actions and to apologize when appropriate. Lastly, it is important to understand how and when to use praise.

Keep in mind that you may be changing how you interact with your child if you incorporate these techniques into your conversations. Children often feel off-balance when parents try something new because they don't know the new "rules." To get your children on board and to prevent them from feeling that you're manipulating them, it would be wonderful to have a discussion with your kids where you say that you're going to try to start talking so that you can be nicer and more positive.

Your children will likely be surprised and pleased that you think enough of them and your relationship with them to try and change your behavior. The younger the child is, the more quickly and enthusiastically he will respond to your new communication style. Toddlers and preschoolers may not even remember a time before you communicated this way, and it will rapidly become your household norm. Preteens and teenagers may make fun of you using these skills, but they will appreciate them and will slowly begin to use them as well.

- **Mirroring: Non-Judgmental Acceptance of Your Child's Feelings**

The first and most basic communication skill that will help you better communicate with your child is mirroring. Mirroring is when you repeat back what your child has said. In the case of a pre-verbal child, you say what you think they mean. Here is an example of mirroring. Your eight-year-old says to you, "You never let me do anything! Daddy lets me watch TV for two hours every night!" You would simply respond, "You feel like I don't let you do anything, and Daddy lets you watch TV every night." This makes your child feel understood, and, even more importantly, it stops you from responding in one of these typical, unhelpful ways:

Defensiveness: "Well, Daddy doesn't have to do homework with you!"

Counterattack: "Maybe with Daddy, you act nicer!"

Dismissing: "Yeah right, he tells me he limits you to an hour."

The purpose of mirroring is to show your child that you understand his point. This is the basic foundation for a calm discussion. If you show your child that you at least hear what he is saying, your child will not escalate the situation as rapidly, if at all. Many children calm down immediately and expand on what they mean. Mirroring is easy once you get the hang of it. Best of all, you can usually see your child's relief when, instead of correcting her or defending yourself, you just repeat what she has said without judgment.

- **Empathy**

Empathy is the basis of all intimate interpersonal relationships. When you empathize with someone, you truly understand her perspective, no matter whether or not you agree with her thoughts or opinions. Empathy, if expressed well, instantly defuses even the most explosive, high-conflict situation.

It can be relationship-changing, but it can also be challenging, especially when you're under stress, or you're trying to empathize with someone you don't understand at all. We will explore how to empathize with your kids in a variety of situations, particularly those times when you're feeling frustrated, anxious, and angry, and especially when your child is doing things that you find incomprehensible. Once you master the skill of empathizing, you can use it in any situation that arises where you want to connect to your child or defuse conflict.

Empathizing is the first step in addressing your children's intense emotional reactions, or their difficult, destructive, or otherwise frustrating behavior. This flies in the face of how the majority of parents respond when a child acts upset. Generally, when parents see their kids acting extremely upset or behaving "badly," the parents feel distressed, angry and powerless. They try to jump right in and remedy things, often by telling kids they shouldn't feel or act that way, problem-solving, telling their kids about alternate ways that they can behave, and even giving them consequences or punishments to help them "shape up."

Although less sensitive or easier-going children will comply with demands, even with a smile, these efforts often go poorly. This is because there is no foundation of empathy, and your child does not feel that you understand his experience. If your child doesn't feel understood, he is less likely to listen to your solutions, try any of your alternative behaviors, or learn anything from the consequences. Instead, he will detach from you, assuming that you have no idea what he feels or thinks. He may also feel alone, sad, angry, and unloved.

- **Be Curious**

If you have no idea how your child is feeling, ask her directly, with warm curiosity. Curiosity is a wonderful and flattering way to make a child, or anyone, feel that her thoughts and feelings are interesting to you. Express your curiosity openly, like:

"I'm interested in what you're feeling, but I don't think I understand."

"I'm curious about what you are/were feeling."

"I've never been in this situation. How do you feel?"

In all of these examples, the key is that you are not judging your child for not communicating effectively, or, worse, for having feelings that don't make sense.

- **Validation**

To fully understand validation, we have first to use empathy. As you just read, empathy means acknowledging and understanding another person's thoughts and feelings. Validating takes this understanding one step further, as you are now saying that it makes sense to you that the person feels that way. Once you're primed to try to validate your child, you may even be able to think of additional reasons why your child's emotion is logical given the situation. Remember, to validate your child, and you do not have to say that you'd react the same way. You do have to say that it makes sense to you that your child, in your child's unique situation, feels the way that he does.

- **Don't Compare**

Often, parents who experienced divorce as children themselves are committed to making their divorce an easier experience for their kids. They try to keep the divorce as conflict-free as possible and to keep their child's routines intact. Then, they often feel bewildered and hurt when their children are just as angry, sad, and accusatory as they were toward their parents, and even significantly more so!

If you are a child of divorce, don't fall into the trap of assuming that you and your child are undergoing identical experiences. Comparing your experiences, feelings, and reactions to your child can often backfire, especially if you feel that you coped more effectively, or if you believe your situation was more difficult.

Another common occurrence is the downward parental comparison. It is easy to think of your divorce as a minimal stressor on your child if you were sexually abused by an alcoholic parent, or had a parent die when you were very young. If you were caring for your younger siblings as a teenager because your mother suffered from debilitating depression, it is likely to anger you when your teenage child complains about waiting another year to get his car.

There is no chance that your child will learn new coping skills because he has heard that you, at his age, were able to cope well. You have likely already witnessed the emotional shutdown and retreat that occur when you tell your child how good he has it compared to you. However, many parents keep reiterating this information in the unrealistic hope that, one day, their child will try to change his behavior to be more like theirs. If your child could cope better with the divorce, he already would be. Hearing how responsible, well-behaved, and appreciative, you were as a child will either seem like a lie to your child or make him feel like a failure in your eyes and his own. Lastly, if your child feels that he will always be compared to you and will come up short, he will withdraw and prefer not to engage at all. This way, he can avoid being compared unfavorably to you and facing your disappointment.

Most kids in divorced families are unsure about how much you want to hear them talk about their other parent. Even if you are extraordinarily angry with your co-parent, you need to show your child that she can discuss her other parent with you openly, without you responding negatively. Remember, if your child is led to reject one parent, she is rejecting half of herself, and her self-esteem will suffer accordingly. As a child ages, she can make her judgments about what qualities she likes and wants to emulate from both you and her other parent, but at this age, it is healthiest for your child to view both parents as positive overall.

It is natural to want to be your child's favored parent. But hearing that your child dislikes or feels hurt by your co-parent can be even more upsetting. It is best to take a neutral attitude toward your co-parent when speaking to your child.

Chapter 9. Parenting Schedule and Importance of Routines

Kids love to celebrate. That love of celebration doesn't change after divorce, but children of divorce may be more apprehensive about it. At this stage, your children are getting used to living in two homes, and if there is a celebration coming up, you can bet they're worried about it. Who will attend? Whose house will be? Will their parents argue or ignore each other? Will there be one celebration or two? No matter what, this is about your children, not you and your co-parent. Keep the focus on them and remain flexible.

When it comes to holidays, you will ideally have built a holiday schedule into your parenting plan. Perhaps you and your co-parent will spend different holidays with your children on alternate years.

For example, if your co-parent has the children for Thanksgiving, maybe you will have the children that year for another holiday, and then switch the following year. Find what works for both of you. For example, if you are Christian, this may mean that you'll miss those opening gifts first thing on Christmas morning for some years. Other religions have their own but similar traditions, and likewise, you may miss participating in traditional observances on the actual date on alternate years. However, you can still maintain the tradition even if it doesn't happen on an exact day.

When it comes to one-time events such as religious milestones and graduations, know that what's most important is that your children feel special. It doesn't matter if they're going home with your co-parent afterward; you can celebrate their achievements on another day. The most important thing is that both of you are at a special event to support your children.

Toddlers

Toddlers handle changes to the schedule best when they know what to expect. Though celebrations are exciting, they still need to know what's going to happen to enjoy them fully. Tell your child who is likely to be at a celebration and what will likely occur. If you and your co-parent have a high-conflict relationship, it's best to keep celebrations separate. If you believe that both you and your co-parent and your friends and family can get along for your toddler's sake, then it may work to create one celebration for them.

Preschoolers

Preschoolers love celebrations. An upcoming celebration will keep them filled with anticipation for days! Just like their toddler counterparts, communicate what you can to your preschooler to ease any anxiety they may have about the event. If you are creating one celebration for your preschooler, share the guest list with them if you are completely sure those people are attending. For example, be sure that your co-parent is coming to an event before telling your preschooler they will be there. If the co-parent does not show up, it will be tough for your preschooler to understand.

Young Children

How celebrations look starts to change a bit with young children. For example, this age group often celebrates birthdays with large parties and invites the entire class. If this is the case and you feel that you and your co-parent can get along, it's a great opportunity for both of you to document the fun they have with their friends. If you are not able to attend together, the co-parent who is attending should share photos with the other co-parent. Co-parents can host this party in alternate years, so neither one feels left out.

Preteens

Remember that your preteens are very social. This means that they will want to celebrate their birthday with their friends. While it's essential to have family involved, your preteens' focus will be on when they can get together with their peers. Try to compromise with your co-parent, if necessary, to make this possible for your children. When it comes to celebrating with family, will you host a single birthday party, or will each family celebrate their birthday?

Though holidays are generally reserved for family time, preteens will likely be checking in with their friends on their phones or tablets on the day of the holidays. When it's time to celebrate with the family, ask them to put away the electronics so you can be present with each other.

Teenagers

Birthdays for teenagers are more about their friends than they are about you. Many divorced parents find that birthday celebrations with their teenagers are done separately simply because teenagers' lives are so focused on friendships.

Young Adults

When it comes to smaller events like birthdays for young adults, you can celebrate them whenever it works for you and your children. You and your co-parent can each celebrate separately with your children unless there is a special tradition you've shared for years that you agree to continue. Perhaps you and your co-parent will keep that tradition alive with some tweaks so that it can be celebrated separately.

The holiday schedule is more flexible with young adults. Perhaps they will split the holiday between their parents. For example, maybe they will have Thanksgiving lunch with one family and Thanksgiving dinner with another. Or perhaps they will alternate holidays between parents. Your young adult probably has thoughts about what they would like to do, so check in with them.

Aside from graduation, the most significant events you'll have with your young adult are engagement parties and weddings. These are events neither parent should miss. Speak to your children about how you and your co-parent can make them feel comfortable.

Discipline Dos and Don'ts

One of the many ways to help your children feel safe is keeping them accountable for what they do. Though no child will willingly line up for grounding or removal of screen time, if they aren't disciplined, they will feel a sense of insecurity.

Regardless of how old their children are, many parents feel like they need to overcompensate for the divorce. They ease up on rules and expectations and don't feel like they need to follow through on consequences. Please understand that the security that comes with a consistent set of rules and consequences is irreplaceable. It would be like your children returning to school after winter break only to discover that the rules they'd been following had changed because the teacher feels bad for them. There would be chaos, and their ability to learn would suffer. The same applies to the home. Here are a few rules for co-parents to follow no matter the age of their children:

- **Wherever possible, decide together on what the rules and expectations should be.**

If you cannot decide, work with a parenting expert in your community to help you develop this part of the parenting plan. While you work with them, decide on the consequences you will both follow through. Then comes the important part: both parents need to follow through. This should be part of your parenting plan, but if it's not, it's never too late to add it.

- **Communicate what is happening with your children to your co-parent.**

Your co-parent can't back you up and present a united front if they don't know what's happening.

- **Keep your cool as much as possible.**

Sometimes parents need to put themselves in a timeout when misbehavior rears its head. If you discipline in anger, your co-parent would have to follow your lead to present a united front and vice versa. It's easier to continue the united front if you both recognize the frustration and take a mental break before disciplining.

- **Be consistent.**

If you expect your co-parent to follow your lead, you need to follow theirs. Your children will know where the crack is if one of you does not follow through and use it to get out of consequences. It makes your co-parent's life hard and ensures your children never have to listen to the rules.

When you have a high-conflict relationship, or you cannot agree on disciplining, using a phrase like, "I know your mom/dad doesn't do this, but I do" can help you remain an authority figure in your children's eyes even if you are not on the same page with your co-parent. Your consequences can carry over even if your children leave for time with their other parent. Be clear and tell your children, "You have lost an hour of screen time for the next five days you are with me."

Remember that you are building new routines at this point in your divorce along with new ways to discipline. Some of those routines will become traditions your children will cherish for years. And though a lot in their lives has changed, not everything has to. You will continue to be there for them for the important times and will continue to celebrate their achievements and special events. Support and encourage involvement from your co-parent in whatever way works for your family. Your children simply want to know they are special in the eyes of both of their parents.

Chapter 10. Healing from Emotional Abuse

Emotional abuse is deeply damaging, and without going through the healing process, you become even more vulnerable to entering into the same type of relationship. You have been violated psychologically, and you will experience anxiety, depression, and dissociation, feelings of low self-esteem, low self-worth, nightmares, and flashbacks. You must seek counseling to assist you in the healing process; however, there are strategies you can implement in your daily life that will help you to move forward.

Exercise

Whether it's going for long intensive walks, going for a jog, join a dance class, or joining the gym, incorporating exercise into your daily routine will help during the healing process. If you don't have any motivation, don't try and do too much at once; for example, you can start by going for a ten-minute walk and then increase it as time goes on. Exercise lowers cortisol levels and releases endorphins, which helps to replace the biochemical addiction you developed with your abuser with something that will benefit you. This addiction was formed through chemicals such as cortisol, dopamine, serotonin, and adrenaline, which strengthen the bond with your abuser and form the cycle of highs and lows. Exercise allows you to build a wall of strength and resilience after leaving an abuser. It also helps to eliminate many physical problems associated with the abuse, such as weight gain, sleep problems, premature aging, and a depleted immune system.

Yoga

Yoga is a combination of physical activity and mindfulness that helps to establish and restore balance. Research has proven that yoga alleviates anxiety and depression. It improves symptoms of post-traumatic stress disorder in victims of domestic violence, boosts self-esteem, and improves body image. Yoga involves a series of powerful movements that compensate for the feelings of powerlessness that victims of abuse are left with.

Meditation

Trauma disrupts the area in the brain responsible for memory, learning, emotion regulation, and planning. The research found that meditation benefits the same areas of the brain that are affected by trauma, such as the hippocampus, the amygdala, and the prefrontal cortex. Meditation gives abuse victims their psyche back. It heals the brain and allows them to respond to life from a place of empowerment instead of trauma.

Daily meditation practice strengthens the neural pathways in the brain and boosts grey matter density in areas of the brain related to the fight or flight response and emotion regulation. Meditation also allows you to become aware of your need to make contact with your abuser. When victims are not aware of this, they make an impulse decision, which usually leads to them returning to the relationship. It also makes you more aware of your emotions in general.

Anchor Yourself

In general, emotional abuse survivors have been gaslighted into believing that they were imagining the abuse they were experiencing. You must start anchoring yourself into the reality that you were abused, but you are no longer in that abusive situation. It is common for abuse victims to idealize their relationship and spend time thinking about what could have been if only they were capable of pleasing their partner. Connecting to reality also helps when struggling with mixed emotions towards your abuser. As mentioned, one of the strategies of the narcissist is to show affection and withdraw it, and it is the affectionate side of the narcissist that victims are drawn to. The narcissist seeks to erode the reality of their victim, but once you reconnect with your reality, you can see your abuser for who he truly is.

To start the anchoring process, make a list of ten of the most abusive incidents that took place during your relationship. When you get tempted to reconnect with your abuser, read this list and remind yourself of how evil he was to you, how he degraded you, and made you feel less than human. You can also write down statements about how he made you feel, such as: "My abuser made me feel that I wasn't worth anything." "My abuser made me feel depressed." "My abuser made me feel that I was stupid." "My abuser made me feel as if I was getting what I deserved and that no one could ever love me the way he did." Remind yourself of these feelings any time you are tempted to pick up the phone and call him or go to his house and see him. Ask yourself whether it feels good for someone to make you believe this about yourself. The more you remember the negative feelings associated with the relationship, the easier it will be to stay away.

Learn to Love Yourself

This might sound cliché, but it is essential if you are going to move on with your life and eventually get into a healthy relationship. When you love yourself, you know who you are and what you stand for. No one can come along and try to convince you that you are anything less than the best. When you develop a certain level of confidence and self-worth, nothing can shake you. Here are some tips on how to love yourself after an abusive relationship:

- **Get in Shape**

When you look good, you feel good. Make a decision not only to improve your health but to transform your body. Whatever your ideal weight and shape are, aim for that.

- **Change Your Wardrobe**

Once you have achieved your ideal body shape, treat yourself to some new clothes. You don't need to break the bank but buy some signature pieces that are really going to make you feel good about yourself.

- **Have Fun Alone**

do something that you enjoy. A lot of abuse victims have difficulty being alone, which is why they are such easy prey for abusers. Spending time alone will teach you how to enjoy your own company. Things you could do might include going to the movies, out to dinner, or finding a new hobby.

- **Try Something New**

Do things that you wouldn't normally do. Try something new and crazy like skydiving or bungee jumping. That's a bit extreme, but you know yourself better than anyone else, so you can choose something that you know will add an element of surprise to your life.

- **Go on Vacation**

Even if you don't make it a regular thing, take a vacation somewhere. Go to a country that's entirely out of your comfort zone. If you are afraid to go alone, invite a friend. Experience a different culture, new food, various activities, and have fun.

- **Journal**

Journaling is an excellent way to release any negative emotions you are feeling. It is also a good way of tracking your progress. When you come out of an abusive relationship, you will have more bad days than good ones. But after some time, you will notice that your emotions will begin to stabilize.

- **Learn to Say No**

Being submissive is a survival mechanism for women in abusive relationships. You would never dare say no to your partner in fear of what might happen. However, now that you are not in an abusive relationship, you mustn't carry this submissive nature into your friendships or feel as if you need to say yes to everyone to please them. This will rob you of your energy and time to yourself.

- **Celebrate Your Accomplishments**

No matter how small you think the accomplishment is, celebrate it. Going through a whole day without thinking about your ex is an accomplishment, and being consistent with your daily exercise routine is an accomplishment. Please pay attention to these things and treat yourself for it.

- **Challenge Yourself**

Is there anything that you have always wanted to do, but you have never gotten around to doing it? Make a list of these things and start doing them. You may have always wanted to compete in a triathlon or to get some additional qualifications. Decide that whatever you put your mind to, you are going to achieve.

- **Learn to Trust Yourself**

Your instincts told you that something wasn't right before you got into an abusive relationship, but you chose to ignore them and pursue the relationship in the hopes that things would get better. Familiarize yourself with that feeling, because any time something isn't right, that is how you will feel, and this isn't just about relationships, it's in all areas of your life.

Chapter 11. How to Give the Best Guidance to Your Child

You have learned that taking things personally and losing your control feeds into your narcissistic ex's behavior. They will continue to do things to spite you, manipulate you or your children, and always have their own best interests at heart, not your child's. By limiting contact, setting parental guidelines, providing structure for yourself, modeling healthy communication, and ignoring the narcissist's attempts to abuse you, you can focus more on your child. In this co-parenting situation, your child's development is of crucial importance.

Encourage Individuality

Children are influenced by everything and everyone in their world. A narcissist will make them believe that they have to please everyone or "bow down" to their peers to feel loved or appreciated. The child of a narcissist is not an individual, but a reflection of them. You, being the non-narcissistic parent, can counteract these habits by helping your child realize that they are their person. As all children like to follow their parent's lead, make sure to model positive mannerisms to help them figure out the difference between 53 impolite behavior and kindness. Seek opportunities for your child to grow independently, such as:

- Providing creative activities

- Asking them which sports or summer camp they would like to join

- Journaling their thoughts and feelings

- Letting them choose their clothes and toys

Encourage Self-Esteem

Self-esteem is built through unconditional love and acknowledgment. Build positive reinforcement through the milestones your child accomplishes in their lives. Give them praise when it's needed, not when they do something to gain your affection. Narcissists have a high, self-absorbed image and so their love will only ever be conditional as long as your child serves them and their needs. More ways to counteract this are:

- Tell your child that they are smart or good (when they are good) to remind them that they have good traits.

- Praise them for things like going potty on their own, winning third place at the fair, or displaying good behavior with their friends.

- Be careful with what you say to them, like, "you are so awesome in my eyes" rather than "you are the most awesome person in the whole wide world."

Help Build Self-Confidence

Your child is always taking in new information and building skills to boost their self-confidence and reward them by saying things like "wow, you are good at that, show me again." Or "some things take practice, why don't we try again?" In doing this, you allow your child to figure out what their strengths and weaknesses are, which encourages independence and teaches them to develop confidence in the things they can do while letting go of perfecting what they can't. Try this:

- Sign your child up for a sports team

- Encourage them to try new things

- Explain that being fearful is their body's way of reacting to change and that change is a good thing

Allow Mistakes to Be Opportunities

A narcissistic parent will make sure that their child strives to be the best and only rewards them when they are the best. This promotes perfectionism and results in temper tantrums when your child can't impress. Teach your child:

Mistakes will happen but are needed to grow into happy individuals.

Make a mistake on purpose in front of your child, and don't make it a big deal. Like paint together and "accidentally" color out of the lines. Say oops and laugh about it.

Challenge them to things they don't enjoy doing or are not good at doing, then applaud their efforts and say "good job for trying."

Do not exaggerate their accomplishments, as focusing too much on this can put pressure on them, which encourages perfectionist behavior.

Create Positive Influences and Environments for Your Child

Creating a stable environment for your child, one where they will feel safe, secure, and confident, will keep their minds at ease during the switch between parents. As hard as this is on you to co-parent with your ex, it is even harder on your children to adapt to such change. Building a community of support can help aide you in this difficult transition. This can also help your child make positive connections and learn from others, not just you.

Teaching your child empathy

All children and teens are selfish individuals, which is part of their development to independence and individuality. However, it doesn't become a problem unless there is no remorse or feelings behind their actions. You can teach them empathy by:

- Always remind them that other people have feelings, too.

- When reading or watching TV, ask your child how they think the person feels.

- When your child does something good or bad to someone else, ask them how they would feel if it had been done to them. This will help them realize the other person's feelings.

Explaining the importance of friends and family

Narcissists are usually lonely and sheltered. They rarely have friends come over, and they rarely let their child have play dates. Children can pick up on these patterns and use their friends in the same way through manipulation or exploitation. To counteract this:

- Inspire your child to make healthy bonding relationships.

- Role model healthy interaction.

- Host get-together and invite friends for your child while modeling laughter and fun times.

- Demonstrate loyalty, sharing, and effective communication skills.

Discipline and explain manipulation tactics used by your child

Every child will push limits and boundaries to see what they can and cannot get away with. This is where positive reinforcement and discipline comes in. Catch their malicious acts, pull them aside, and explain at eye level how unhealthy this type of communication is. Explain to them a better way to handle the situation and ignore or overlook negative tantrums. When you feed into the positive, you develop positive attitudes. When you give attention to the anger and negativity, it allows them to continue because even though throwing hissy fits, they are still getting a reaction out of you.

- If your child tries to manipulate their friend by saying, "if you don't do xxx, I won't xxx,"

Catch their behavior and tell them that holding something over someone else's head is inappropriate and will not be tolerated. Let them know that they cannot control someone else, but they can do their own thing if their friend isn't playing nicely.

- A role model to them that the kinder you are, the more beneficial rewards you will get.

- Explain to them that through effective communication and being polite, people will likely want to help you rather than if they fear you.

- Every time they do something positive on their terms, later, pull them aside and tell them how proud you are of handling the situation the way they did.

Chapter 12. Loving Again

Dating is not exciting for your children. They want to process this divorce and spend healthy, quality time with you for at least the first year. Take dating slow and easy; you have a posse behind you now (your kids). Another person adds an extra dynamic that your children have to deal with. They are dealing with enough right now.

When you begin to date, your kids are counting on you to do so wisely. You have to be sure this is a good person for you and then assess if they are also good for your children. The truth is they can be good for you and not your kids (jealous of your kids, different parenting styles, don't really like kids, etc.). When you were single without kids, dating was different. You are now a parent whose number one job is to protect your children and keep them safe. You must pay close attention to the behaviors of the person you are dating. If you see anything that you do not feel is healthy, take more time to assess this person before introducing them to your children (or simply quickly ending the relationship), so your kids are not put through another unhealthy relationship or divorce.

The other important point to understand is that your children may grow attached to this person. If you break up with your partner, your children will suffer another loss. This can be hard for them, and it can be another opportunity for them to blame themselves. This is important to understand, so you can communicate with your children about their feelings if you do end a future relationship.

Two Rules for Dating Before Introducing Your New Dating Partner to Your Child:

1. It has been one year since you officially divorced or separated (separated means you have been living in different homes and your children know you are getting divorced).

Why this is important: Your children must go through the grief cycle before they are ready to meet anyone new in your life. The grief cycle is twelve to eighteen months. You also need time alone with your children to develop your relationship with them.

Child's Perspective: "I feel like my dad is trying to replace my mom, and I don't like that". Girl, age 8. Your kids have a mom and a dad; they don't need another new parent right now.

2. You have dated your new dating partner for at least three months.

Why this is important: You must have time to assess this new partner before introducing them to your children. New dating partners can feel stressful for your child, and you want to minimize the number of people you introduce to them. Children can get attached to new people, and if the relationship then ends, they can feel another loss.

Child's Perspective: "I did not have a mom in my life, so every time my dad brought someone home, I was sure she was going to be my new mommy, but usually after about three to six months she would leave, and I would be heartbroken that my new mom left once again, this happened so many times in my life.". Twenty-year-old female

8 Great Habits to Start Your New Relationship the Right Way

- **Slow and steady**

Hold back when you meet someone new. Remember, if they are the ones you have all the time in the world to enjoy that fact. If they are not, you should enjoy the relationship for what it is and protect yourself so you don't have to heal and recover from a disastrous relationship.

- **Communicate**

Set the tone for the relationship you would like to have with someone by being that person yourself. Be kind. Be on time. Communicate as clearly as you can. A new relationship is a fresh start, and you can steer it in the right direction by being respectful and positive.

Even when arguments come along—and they will—remember that you have something special between you and you need to look after that, even if you are having a temporary disagreement. It's possible to fight with someone while remaining respectful and not doing any permanent damage to the bond between you.

If it's meant to be, you'll have set the groundwork for a rich and loving relationship by treating your partner as you would like to be treated.

- **Focus on the other person**

To build a strong relationship takes time and effort. It's often the result of many daily interactions, and learning to focus on someone and respond to them is a useful skill for any relationship, not just a romantic one.

To do this, first of all, eliminate distractions. Make time to spend with your partner, switch off screens, listen, and focus. Even if you are busy and rushing off in separate directions, eye contact and affection can go a long way toward maintaining a healthy and loving connection.

- **Look after yourself**

Just because you've met someone new, this doesn't give you an excuse to stop your efforts to heal from your experience with a narcissist. Keep doing all those things you did to recover—talking to a therapist, looking after your physical and mental wellbeing, journaling, and spending time alone to rest and recharge. Taking time to reflect on where the relationship is going and how you are feeling is another way of looking after yourself as you move forward.

Even in the early days, get in the habit of setting aside some personal space, even if you feel like being with them all the time. Give them time to miss you and feel curious about what you've been up to. It's important to give yourself time to enjoy your own company.

- **Don't dwell in the past**

Whatever happened with the narcissist, don't let yourself dwell too much on it if it makes you feel bad. You need to spend some time on it, either alone or with a therapist, but don't live there. When you find yourself ruminating or wondering how the narcissist is going, bring yourself firmly back into the present with self-care or distraction.

On this note, don't assume that all of your future partners are going to let you down. If you have done some work on yourself and reflected on what may have led you to your narcissistic partner, you should be able to avoid carrying this baggage into your new relationship. Give this new person a chance.

- **Remind yourself of how far you have come**

Remember that you got yourself away, you are now safe, and you have a lot to look forward to.

If you find yourself regretting the time you spent with them, remind yourself that you have a whole future ahead of you that they no longer have the power to ruin. You are safe. You deserve to be happy.

- **Don't badmouth the relationship to others**

If you are starting with someone, it's sometimes a good idea to let it grow in its own time, and in private, before you start talking about it too much to others. It's natural to want to share your new relationship with friends, but just be mindful of how much you share. Try to keep some things private. There are a couple of reasons for this.

First, letting others into your new world with this person too quickly, particularly if they prefer you single, can harm the new relationship. Secondly, talking about the relationship in detail with others has a way of taking away energy from its growth and opening up the new bond you have formed to the influence of others, who may not have your best interests at heart.

If you aren't sure about how it's going but generally feel OK, talk to your new partner, or your journal, or your therapist. And if you feel suddenly upset, don't go rushing off to badmouth your new partner to your friends. A new relationship is fragile, like a seedling or tiny baby, and you need to treat it well as it grows stronger.

• Laugh together

Sharing humor is one of the best ways to relieve stress and bond with your partner. And it's what makes being in a relationship with someone so much fun. So don't forget to laugh, enjoy each other's company, and be silly together.

As you move on from the narcissist, remember to be positive and hopeful for the future, but also realistic. Unfortunately, there are some people out there you need to steer well clear of for your wellbeing and happiness. But many others will enrich your life. Ultimately, it's about finding that sweet spot between keeping yourself safe and trusting in those that you meet to do the right thing by you. If the relationship you've had with a narcissist is good for anything, it's that you have learned how to look after yourself in new ways. Believe in your new insights, get out there, and have fun.

Chapter 13. Tips for Recovery

Although narcissistic abuse does have long-term effects, that doesn't mean that you will never be able to overcome those effects. The psychological and emotional wounds of narcissistic abuse will heal with time, as long as you give them the chance to do so. Even the impact of abuse on your brain can be reversed as you recover. Like a broken bone growing back stronger than before, you may also find that your new self is healthier and more resilient than the person you were before you suffered the abuse.

Waking Up

The first stage in healing is to understand how narcissistic personality disorder develops and what narcissism means. A lot of things that seemed complicated and confusing should make a lot more sense once you understand and accept this. For example, you may have wondered how your partner could be so kind, loving, and attentive in some situations and so unpredictable, cruel, and undermining others. Both behaviors were merely expressions of your partner's underlying narcissism, which drives him to interact with others in a pattern that is much more predictable than you may have realized:

- Idealization: in this phase, the narcissist projects all his fantasies about ideal love and support onto the new person in his life, giving them the false impression that he can heal their wounds and securing a new source of narcissistic supply.

- Devaluation: in this phase, the narcissist projects all his inner fears, self-hatred, and insecurities onto another person, destroying their sense of self. He may return to the idealization phase temporarily to keep his victim hooked, but he will always come back to the devaluation phase in a little while.

- Discarding: in this phase, the narcissist finds someone else to provide him with narcissistic supply and abandons the previous victim, often without warning.

Not many people will leave the narcissist in the idealization phase; it only feels too good, especially for someone with unresolved childhood wounds. Generally speaking, only experts at spotting narcissists will recognize this stage for what it is and escape in time.

Many people will only leave once they are well into the devaluation phase and have already suffered a lot of damage. Many don't leave even then and are blind-sided when the narcissist leaves them for someone else. Either way, the first stage of healing is waking up: recognizing the narcissist for what he is.

Highly empathic people are potentially vulnerable to narcissists for several reasons. One reason is that the childhood experiences that produce codependency also tend to produce children highly attentive to the emotions of the people around them. Another reason is the nature of empathy itself. If you're always the one who can see the other side of the story, if you're willing to meet people halfway, if you still want to understand and forgive, you will find it harder to face the harsh truth about it the narcissist.

Breaking Contact

Ending your relationship with the narcissist is an important step, but it will be hard to maintain unless you go all the way. Completely breaking contact is essential for healing because otherwise, the narcissist will do everything within his power to maintain control.

For example, if you move out of your abuser's house but stay in contact by phone, he will still have the ability to use almost every tactic in his manipulative repertoire. Even if you're determined not to go back to him, he can get a power thrill by saying something he knows will push your buttons. The same is true if you remain in contact by email or if he keeps sending you messages through friends or family members. He may try to win you back with empty promises, or he may just try to hurt you or make you mad.

If you want to start healing as soon as possible, it's essential to break contact with the narcissist completely. Refuse to see him. Don't answer his phone calls. Delete his emails without reading them. Block his texts. Tell friends and family members who are still in contact with him that you aren't interested in getting any messages.

Along with breaking off all contact, resist the urge to check up on him or see how he's doing. Even glancing at his social media pages would be a mistake. He's most likely to post pictures of himself having a great time with someone else to make you jealous or ranting about how much you've mistreated him or anything else he thinks might trigger an emotional reaction.

It's not easy to do this, but your goal should be not only to cut off all contact with the narcissistic abuser but to remove every last thread connecting their life to yours, including your thoughts.

To defend yourself from continued abuse in this situation, limit your contact to the bare minimum required by the court-ordered custody agreement. These agreements often allow you to specify the type and frequency of contact. For instance, you may be able to require your co-parent to call the children only at scheduled times or to refrain from contacting you except by email.

Some family courts can appoint a Guardian ad Litem to safeguard your children's legal interests, or a Parent Coordinator to handle scheduling issues and any necessary communication. Whatever the specific arrangements, make sure your custody agreement spells everything out in as much detail as possible and leaves no room for ambiguity.

Resist the urge to ask your children about your former partner, and never ask your children to carry messages for you. Even if it isn't easy to break off all contact, you need to get as close as possible to no-contact to heal.

Go no contact. Rid yourself of the toxicity of the relationship. This will free your mind, so you can grieve, assess your situation, make life changes, heal, and grow as an individual. With the abusive narcissistic still lingering, it is difficult to get a clear head.

Acknowledge THIS WAS NOT YOUR FAULT. The narcissist's key tactic is to avoid and deviate from responsibility while dumping this on you. Take a sigh of relief and rest in this notion. You didn't cause this to happen, didn't deserve this to happen, and do not merit being abused by a narcissist.

Take Responsibility

Step back and take a bird's eye view of your relationship. Were there red flags or did something that appeared off in the relationship? Think about this and assess it.

Set up time with a professional counselor or therapist that specializes in narcissistic abuse. Make sure the counselor truly understands the situation. If you feel the counselor is trying to blame you for the abuse, or feel the need to defend what happened and don't feel it's safe, find another counselor or therapist.

Realize your friends and family may not be supportive. Your friend and family may not be the ones you confide in and discuss the recovery. They just may not understand. As you search for validation, know this is the place where it may not be found.

Realize there are stages of grief, and each stage takes time.

Take a Break from Social Media

As your friends and family's lives are going on as normal and are posting their pictures at the beach, and family vacation, and weekend events, it may be best to take a break from the lives people portray on social media. Take care of your emotional well-being and find another activity to engage in that will heal your mind from the emotional rollercoaster you experienced.

Block your narcissistic abuser on your phone for text and email. Do not respond. Keep in mind the abuser will send flying monkeys to try and contact you.

As you heal, this is a time for inner development and restoration. I recommend you take a long break from Facebook and social media. It is reported that many everyday users report depression after using Facebook. As you are going through a unique healing time, use this time to take a break, a hiatus, for an extended time to cleanse your soul, restore your personality, create and re-establish new passions, enhance your vision for your future, weep, grieve, and have devoted times to yourself and your needs which have been neglected for so long.

It may be tempting to engage in conversation over social media regarding your narcissist ex or common friends. Resist the urge, disengage, and take a mental break.

Realize that the narcissistic abuser will send flying monkeys to you to question and will test your new boundaries. This may be difficult as some flying monkeys may also be your friends. This has to be evaluated closely to see their true intention.

Get a New Pet

As you recover, a great new furry friend may be the best thing for you. Pets have a way of showing unconditional love to us.

Realize that there will come a time when you are healed. The recovery process may take a while, and that is okay. Go through the stages.

Now that you are beautiful, fun and these qualities do not have to be broadcasted on Facebook for everyone to be aware of how special you are. Go through the process to receive inner peace with yourself and circumstances. Develop a new identity so that you are fully capable of your skin even with the scars of the past. Now there is a quiet strength that can be birthed, and it carries the qualities of gold in your inner being.

Chapter 14. Mistakes to Avoid on the Road to Recovery

It is not easy to end a relationship with someone who was a part of your life. However, it is about the things you do after ending the relationship, which determines whether you can recover and move on with your life or stay obsessed with the emotional predator and the sad situation. You get to decide whether you want to move ahead or not. You have the control here to free yourself from the burdens of your past. If you're going to regain control of your life and want to move ahead, then there are certain mistakes you must avoid on your road to recovery. Before you learn about the mistakes you must avoid, there are certain things about narcissistic recovery you must keep in mind to move ahead in life.

Please ensure that you don't overwhelm yourself by reading a lot about narcissism and narcissistic recovery. Instead of overwhelming yourself with an excess of information, focusing on the points is a good idea. Please don't ever agree to "staying friends" with the narcissist.

If you are an empathy, you might find it a little tricky to sever all ties with the narcissist. However, take a moment and rationally think about it. How can you ever stay friends with someone who subjected you to narcissistic abuse? Do you think your friends would ever treat you the way the narcissist did? Would you want someone you love and care for to be with a narcissist like you were? If you answer these questions honestly, then you will see that staying friends with the narcissist does you no good whatsoever. Staying in touch with the narcissist will only harm your recovery.

If you have any ideas or are thinking about ways in which you can keep a narcissist in your life, then you need to reconsider it all. You must not allow someone else to ruin your chances of recovery. Severing all ties with the narcissist and putting some physical distance between you and the narcissist is a wonderful idea. Your intentions, regardless of how pure they are, will only give narcissists the idea that the manipulation can go on, and you have no objections. Please don't believe that you will be fully healed when you end the relationship with the narcissist. You will need time and will need to make a conscious effort to heal yourself from the trauma you suffered. Now that we have cleared all this up, it is time to look at some common mistakes you need to avoid at all costs.

The mistake a lot of people make while recovering from narcissistic abuse is their inability to come to terms with the manipulation they were subjected to. At times, victims of narcissistic abuse struggle to accept the fact that the narcissist in their life is not only dangerous to their mental wellbeing but is a threat to their emotional and physical wellbeing.

On the surface of it, no one is fond of the highs, lows, or the uncertainties of life with a narcissist. There comes a time in the life of victims of narcissistic abuse were living with the narcissist becomes a habit to them. They start thinking that the life they live with a narcissist is supposed to be, how they must be, and how they will stay the same. Think of it as an addiction. Your mind will come up with different versions of events and all sorts of reasons as to why you cannot leave the narcissist. You must understand that your reactions need to be based on reality and not your perception of reality. You must stick to the facts, notice all the red flags, and not let anything melt your resolve of breaking all ties with the narcissist.

If you view a situation as being tragic, then you will respond accordingly. If you think of yourself as a victim of circumstances, then that is where you will get stuck. The way you think influences all the choices you make and the way you respond to situations. The moment you feel like you must go out of your way to prove your worthiness to your partner, it is a red flag you cannot afford to ignore. If your partner loves you unconditionally, as they are supposed to, then they know your worth, and you don't have to prove anything. If you are wondering about whether you made the right choice by ending the relationship, think about all the misery and suffering the narcissist subjected you to.

While recovering, people tend to have unrealistic expectations about the time it will take before they can start feeling better. Ending a relationship with a narcissist is quite different from ending a relationship with anyone else in your life. Please don't make the mistake of setting unrealistic goals or expectations about the recovery speed. Who wouldn't want a magic pill that can put an end to all their misery and suffering? Who wouldn't want to wake up in the morning and feel like their usual selves again? Everyone would love this, but alas, there is no such thing as a miracle cure. The process of recovering from narcissistic abuse will take time and effort. Don't lull yourself into thinking that it will be quick and simple. It will take time and effort, but you will feel infinitely better when you recover. If you set any unrealistic expectations for yourself, you are merely setting yourself up for failure.

As much as one would wish for a fairy godmother to fix their situation, recovering from narcissistic abuse is a gradual process. As with any transformation, you were healing yourself is a journey of gradual success, which will take time. The recovery time tends to vary from one person to another. Instant recovery is seldom possible. The process of recovery will take time. It is the amalgamation of several small and practical steps you need to take each day. It is about motivating yourself to move forward instead of getting stuck up in your past, please be kind and patient with yourself.

Victims of narcissistic abuse tend to avoid the hard work of having to move on with their life because they feel like it will make them lose their identity. They feel like they will lose themselves when they end the toxic relationship. For many victims, the process of having to move on causes an identity crisis because the toxic relationship was all they knew about, and it was their life. Regardless of how miserable they were, it was their way of life, and everything they knew would change the minute they decide to move on. The truth is recovery isn't possible unless you want it to happen. Many people stay the way they are because of all the sympathy and pity that comes their way from their loved ones. This tends to make the victims feel like they matter and are worthy of love. So, in their bid to hold onto that feeling, they tend to stay put in toxic relationships.

This kind of thinking seldom does any good, and it will effectively put an end to any recovery you make.

You must answer this question- "Am I ready to allow myself to heal?" Are you ready to take all the steps to heal yourself and move on? Are you willing to make the necessary changes and put in the effort required to free yourself from the narcissist clutches? Don't fear to hit rock bottom. Once you hit rock bottom, the only way is up! Only then will you be able to start recovering from it once you acknowledge the damage you have suffered.

You must understand that you have the right to live your life on your terms. You deserve to live a happy life. You have the right to move away from anything or anyone who harms you in any manner. You deserve to be happy. You deserve to live a life that's free from all forms of abuse. You deserve a chance to grow. You deserve a chance to love and be loved.

Chapter 15. Effects of Narcissistic Abuse over Time

The effects of experience with narcissistic abuse can be devastating and long-lasting. Comorbid conditions like depression and anxiety are common after going through a period of emotional manipulation. They may leave the victim with trust issues and anxieties that last the rest of their lives.

A person may begin to internalize a completely false reality about them, believing them to be flawed fundamentally, undeserving of love, and selfish. The narcissist understands that the more he can make a victim feel like they are doing something wrong, the more he can convince them to do things to correct the error or make up for what they've done. This is especially thrilling because the narcissist realizes that the victim has not done anything wrong; he's that good at manipulation. It is a matter of getting a notch on the belt for narcissism, and the effects on the victim do not garner any guilt or shame from him.

Depression manifests in a prolonged emotional state of hopelessness or helplessness. Many sufferers hear voices in their heads that always tell them they are worthless or stupid or that they are not enough. This voice may manifest as the narcissist's voice himself in a victim of narcissistic abuse. The voice may be persistent for days on end, especially at night, when relaxation becomes impossible.

Anxiety is another possible aftereffect of narcissist abuse and especially common in instances where there is a history of physical abuse as well. The anxiety will often stem from the creation of doubt and destruction of self-esteem that goes along with narcissistic abuse. Whatever a narcissist can sink their teeth into, and they will do it.

Towards the end of the abuse cycle, the victim may finally start to see the light and attempt to get as far away from the perpetrator as possible. This may or may not be successful, depending on what else the narcissist has going on at the time. He may have already found someone else to concentrate on, so you may find some peace, at least until they get bored and see you again. This may initially feel tragic, as you've still got to deal with the cultivated emotional attachment. But soon, you will start to realize that you are a survivor of an abuser, and you are lucky to be free.

One technique many abuse victims utilize after an experience like this is therapy, either in a group or a one-on-one setting. It can be beneficial to talk to others who have been through a similar situation. It is essential to be able to ground yourself in the truth that you were not stupid, immoral, bad, or not enough; you were manipulated, just like the others in your group. Talking to these individuals may go a long way in finding yourself again after a long and dreadful experience of narcissistic abuse.

There are several typical emotions and cycles of thought that victims of narcissistic abuse experience immediately following the end of the relationship. The victim is usually quite tired and worn out, and this may last weeks or even months. Emotional exertion takes a toll, just like muscle exertion. You must try to talk to someone or wrap your mind around the reality that you are not at fault. You are not stupid. Someone who is an expert at emotional manipulation with zero sense of remorse has taken complete advantage of you and your pain.

It is common for the victim to go through feelings of guilt and shame. Let these feelings run their course, but again, it is important to put yourself in an environment that supports the truth that you have survived an ordeal, not committed a horrendous crime.Panic attacks and anxiety may go hand-in-hand for a while after the abuse. Some people get out without experiencing symptoms like this, but others will need to address it through talk therapy or drug therapy.

You will feel a big blow to your self-esteem, which may take some time to build back up again. Try to surround yourself with people who love you and who care for you. You will likely go through all kinds of emotional fallout, and it is good to let it out when you need to. You may feel like crying or screaming or releasing your emotions in some other way. Perhaps, you may find it helpful to join a gym and punch a punching bag for an hour. Whatever you need to do, try to express and release that emotion rather than bottling it up inside of you. This will only make the eventual release much worse and may even cause toxicity and additional emotional and psychological turmoil.

It will be natural to have a desire to think things through and figure him out. But it is important that you not exert too much effort on this, because the actions of a narcissist are contradictory, unreasonable, and sporadic. If the following day they need to make a 180 and do something different, they aren't going to care whether or not it makes sense to you; they'll do it. Don't try to figure them out. They're not worth it. And what's much more important, do not put yourself through the ordeal of thinking you can be a fantastic enough influence that you can change them and not narcissistic anymore. This is a waste of time. And likely they are going to use this as just another opportunity to manipulate you in some way.

Cut your losses and move on. Don't ever look back. You may feel tempted from time to time to try and hunt this person down again. Maybe you want to tell them what they did to you or try and explain what they've done wrong to gain some affection or hint of the things they once showed you at the beginning of the relationship. It is so essential that you realize that it was all an act, a complete façade. It would be best if you let these things go and move forward. And don't convince yourself that all men are awful and not worth the trouble. Relationships are always going to present unique difficulties, but I promise you that finding a partner who is respectful, loving, and who shares interests with you is possible. Don't give up.

Chapter 16. Breaking Free

Although being with a narcissist is a truly horrific and often traumatic experience, breaking free can lead to initial loneliness. You are so used to being with that person, being involved in their stories, games, and a sense of companionship even if it is a twisted and mentally- emotionally abusive companionship; that finally leaving and being free can leave you feeling empty. We need connections, stories, relationships, and various realities to keep us feeling alive and fulfilled.

This is, of course, in itself a beautiful process and fundamentally part of your journey. To be alone is to be all one, content, free, and soulfully happy in your on independence. Once we remove attachments and stories which are no longer good for us, we provide ourselves the space and time for new stories, new realities, and frequencies of being. I once heard the saying that life is like music. Life can be equated with music. We do live in a universe after all! So, loneliness can be overcome by filling yourself with new stories in harmony with your best interests and best possible expression.

Connected to this is a self- recovery, healing, and boundary plan. Boundaries are essential, but so is your discovery of self and self-healing. Below are highly effective ways to overcome loneliness.

Passion Projects

Immerse yourself in a passion project. New hobbies, favorite pastimes, or creating a vision board to align with your dreams and aspirations can all be marvelous gateways back to your true self. Following your greatest joy allows you to overcome loneliness and heal from the sufferings caused by your narcissistic partner. Passion and fire are the sparks of life. They energize and revitalize your inner core, further enabling you to stop feeling isolated or cut off from the world. This is an unfortunate consequence of being the victim of narcissistic abuse or mind manipulations- you may feel disconnected to others on a profound level.

Re-Finding Yourself

Have you ever heard of the saying known thyself? This knows yourself on every level; your intentions, goals, dreams, hidden motivations, and your personality in its entirety. We usually become lost and allow in the illusions and judgments of others when we do not know ourselves. 'The self' is the holistic part of being, the persona, characteristics, and beliefs that make us unique. It is our thoughts, feelings, subtle impressions, emotions, experience, and deeper inner workings, also having a soulful aspect or significance. Recovering from a narcissist and re-finding yourself tie in closely to knowing yourself. It will help you overcome loneliness, but it will also help increase your self- esteem, self- worth, and personal confidence.

Positive Self-Talk and Power Words

Positive self- talk may not initially appear as a form of boundary creating. Self- talk is the conversations we have with ourselves. When we engage in positive self- talk, we open new neural pathways and actively influence the neurons in our brains. These neurons are responsible for the way we think, feel, and respond to people, situations, and experiences. They are also responsible for our communication, both internal with us and external through our interactions with others. Just through positive and mindful self- talk, a natural boundary is created due to the ripple effect thoughts have on inner and external reality. In short, an invisible energy field is created through the power of the mind, thoughts, and subtle intentions exhibited. This hidden energy field is your boundaries.

Self-Affirmations

Self- affirmations are mostly affirmations that can be spoken or thought during meditation or any contemplative activity for great effect. They are best performed as a sort of ritual or daily integrated habit. Taking time to dedicate some minutes to affirmations daily will enable your aura, your electromagnetic energy field to be strengthened and expanded, and your mind strengthened. As the body is a complex and interconnected system, this has a profound effect on your emotions and thus increases your sense of boundaries on many levels. Mental boundaries, emotional boundaries, physical boundaries, and spiritual boundaries are real. Once you begin to develop your boundaries truly, you will realize how 'the same' these all are. Once you strengthen one of your boundary muscles, you can protect yourself from harmful or destructive energy. This includes the intentions and attempted projections of your narcissistic ex.

Emotional Muscles

Strengthening and developing your emotional muscles must be part of your boundary plan. Your emotional resilience, intelligence, and connection are your keys to success. Empathy, intuition, and an advanced to mature emotional connection to both yourself and others (the world around) allow you to stay centered within and aligned to your truth, own reality, and choice to stay clear from narcissistic abuse games of your ex. Emotions can be seen as a muscle, even if figuratively, as they control and shape all of physical reality as we know it. We are essentially emotional creatures, and those who are in tune with their inner empathy (advanced empathy) or higher frequency functioning emotions can influence others and reality powerfully and positively.

Emotional Resilience

Emotional resilience allows you to adapt and respond to stressful or chaotic situations with ease and poise or grace. Your emotional health is strong, and you know yourself well enough not to react. Life's difficulties and challenges can be overcome easily if not effortlessly based on how you can recover, adapt, and change with the tides.

Emotional Intelligence

Emotional intelligence is the capacity to be aware of and in control of your emotions. You can easily express yourself and possess certain wisdom and empathy to you, which reflects in your interactions and communications. Interpersonal relationships can be handled judiciously, fairly and maturely, and you often shine a light on others and situations. Emotional intelligence is a key trait to possess when dealing with a narcissist, specifically during the break-up and letting go period.

Empathy

Empathy allows you to possess all of the other key characteristics to be empathetic. It is to feel what it is like to be another literally or be in another's shoes. This allows you to deal with difficulties or strenuous interactions (with your narcissistic ex) in a compassionate, self- respecting, and wise way. Possessing empathy and seeking ways to develop it allows you to increase your boundaries, making them stronger through your ability to connect with a higher frequency (compassion, patience, empathetic- related qualities, etc.).

Intuition

Intuition is your guiding light and your inner compass. It is also known as your gut or gut feeling and can tell you which path to take or not to take in moments of need. It is also responsible for your instincts, instinctual awareness, emotional wisdom, and ability to know and follow your truth. Intuition connects you to higher wisdom and awareness and your seat of personal power- those strongly connected to their intuition know what to say and when, how to act and respond in each moment, and generally everything that will keep them on course. What better way to enhance and expand your boundaries than to develop, and connect to, your intuition?

Emotional Independence

Emotional independence is a sure way to develop and maintain boundaries. Acquiring this sets you apart from the entanglement you once suffered at the hands of your narcissist other (partner). When you are emotionally independent, you have greater if not a certain chance of being free from mind games, manipulations, narcissistic entrapments, and the general dark motivations and intentions of your ex.

Connecting to Your Spiritual Source

Finally, connecting to your spiritual source should be part of any boundary plan. The extent of this will differ for everyone individually, as everyone will have their limits and be on their journey. A spiritual source can mean many things to many different people; to some, it can be as intense as spending days to weeks on a mountain meditating to a state of deep spiritual enlightenment. To others, it may be a recognized spirit which runs through all life and every living thing. The fundamental point is that connecting to spirituality or your own 'inner spirit,' in any way, can have a profound effect on your strength. Boundaries come from strength, and opening yourself spiritually can make you mentally, emotionally, or physically stronger.

Some examples of connecting to your spiritual source for boundary improvement may include reading spiritual literature or poetry, meditating, engaging in transcendental meditation, going on a spiritual retreat, partaking in an ashram, learning about esoteric or ancient wisdom- of astrology, and connecting to your inner nature and spirit through contemplative and reflective activities.

Chapter 17. How the Narcissistic Partner Damages Children

The effects of narcissism exhibited in the lives of his children. There is a general concept of personal doubt which openly displayed in the children of narcissistic parents. One thing that runs through our minds whenever we talk about parenting is the feature of empathy. In other words, all parents have compassion for those they live with, be it children or their spouses or anybody placed under their care. As a parent, either father or mother, you have to have the feeling for your children.

It makes them feel part of you and appreciate the sense of ownership and belonging. As opposed to a narcissistic parent, he does not have empathy at all. When we compare the two scenarios, we can easily formulate conclusions about what we expect as the outcome or the nature of the children.

There are several effects that we will be explaining that are related to the nature of the children raised by narcissistic parents.

Children Feel That They Are Not Seen or Heard

A child at his stage needs to be listened to and heard for whatever reason by the parent. On the contrary, the nature of the narcissist parent is to be listened to and be heard. It is one man's talk. Here, things are colliding. The question you may ask yourself is who needs to be given attention; a child or a parent?

Lack of Acknowledgment tothe Child's Concerns

Let's take an example of a child who feels weak and low as a result of failing an exam. In this case, as a parent, you need to encourage and motivate your daughter by telling her sweet words like: "you are clever; I know you can make it!" Instead, the parent ends up abusing the child by her mother like: "I knew! That is the best you could achieve. You are so stupid, just like your mother. You can never be sharp like your father." This makes the child feel so demoralized, and the reality of the matter has not been taken in.

On the other hand, the child might have performed poorly due to a lack of proper support from parents, but look at what comes out from the parent!

The Relationship between the Parent and the Child Is Worse Off Than That of a Stranger

To a narcissist parent, a child looks more of an accessory. The child may not feel that the real love of a parent because the parent feels like the child is but an additional asset, just like any other assets he has. There is no sense of blood relationship in this context.

More Focus Will Laid Ont he Returns of a Child Rather Than the Child Himself as a Person

As a child of home, you need to be recognized and appreciated as a person in nature. But for this case, what you do has more value to the parent than who you are to them. They will want to associate you with a daily laborer who works for a certain token.

Children are not assets to their own homes. If they are handled as assets, they will develop repellent characteristics towards the father or the mother who behaves in this crude way.

Children Can Never Trust Their Ability and Emotions Therefore He Will Develop Distrust

When a child is not given a chance to exercise their ability, they grow up knowing that it must be someone else to do it for something to happen. Even if they have a talent, they will never trust in themselves. The talents and other unique abilities lost due to low self-esteem and lack of self-confidence.

It is at home that parents give room to children to exercise their talents and other abilities, and as well, it is the role of the parent to motivate them and nature their talents. If this is not done, children will never have that urge to do anything to perfection.

A Child Will Grow Knowing That Physical Outlook Is Better Compared To Feelings

Since narcissistic parents find more delight in the physical appearance, they will instill this misleading notion to their children who will behave as they do. This is true for any family that children will always learn their first behaviors from their parents. If a parent teaches his child to know that appearance is more important than emotions, you can expect to find a generation of ill-mannered children.

This is so because you cannot trade a person's morals for appearance. The two aspects are very distinctive in that one adds value to an individual, yet the other one accounts for the relationships that a person or a child can make in life.

There Will Be Emotional Emptiness In The Life Of The Child

The child will lack responsible emotions that can aid him in living well with people. He won't grow emotionally.

The Child Might Feel Wasted and Exploited

This is the case where a child compares himself to others. He feels like his talents have been killed, and instead, he has wasted his precious time adoring the parents and doing what pleases the parent. A child will feel some perturbing emptiness, both in skill and other abilities.

The Cause A Lot Of Shame to Their Children

A parent does this so that the children will never think outside the box to be able to stand alone in the future; instead, they have to rely on the parents for guidance and advice. In anything that they do, they feel that children must seek their consent.

The way he may bring shame to his child is by showing how their performances are never up to standard compared to other children. It could be in any sector ranging from academic work, social affairs, or even professionally. He will let them feel bad for their friends, dress code, general lifestyle, personal choices, and likings. A narcissistic parent will always shame the children into gaining precedence in their decision making and general authority over them.

They contend with their children

It loses meaning to contend with your children. The question, in this case, is who is more superior to the other? Who should lead the other? Who are the role model and many other relevant questions? If all these questions are answered, you will find that children have no choice but to submit to the parent's false punitive expedition.

Chapter 18. Stop Being Codependent

It is very easy to become codependent in a relationship with a narcissist, even if you were confident before. It can be always very exhausting to have to cater to their needs for attention. You may wonder why that is, why anyone would let the other person control you as if you were a puppet. Well, it is not voluntary, that is for sure. The narcissist will shower their partner with love and attention to see whether they are also narcissistic or if they will accept that much of attention. Now, we as humans cannot resist the sweetness of affection that someone is giving us.

To stay mentally healthy, you will need to stay away from the things you usually do. You will need to stop pleasing everyone, especially the narcissist, and start taking care of yourself. This may not be easy even to imagine, but eventually, you will be able to distance from being everyone's wish-fulfilling person.

When it comes to relationships, especially with a narcissist, you are expected to make them happy and to cheer for them no matter what. You are expected to be there to support them and to help them in whatever then need help. They expect you to be with them night and day and that you are the one who will keep their spirits high. However, is it possible to rely on one person about everything?

Is it okay to burden anyone with such heavy duties? It is certainly not beneficial for the codependent person, just like it is not beneficial for the narcissist. It can be devastating to the relationship. Therefore, they both need to work on their relationship together so that they can thrive. They need to establish a healthy relationship that will be characterized by a strong bond of mutual respect, happiness, and dependence on both sides. They both need to work on their behaviors so that the narcissist does not rely as much on the codependent, and the codependent does not feel the urge to make everyone happy. You will both probably need help from a therapist to overcome the issues that have been bothering, and that caused you to behave the way you do.

However, there are some things you can do yourself that will help you to be less codependent and even set yourself free. One of them is get reconnected with your friends and family. If you are in a relationship with a narcissist, they have probably insisted in some way that you stop seeing your friends and family. They probably told you many lies so that you would distance from the people who care about you. Therefore, you need to start bonding with them and reconnecting, so that you have a support system that will help you not to rely on your partner as much as you do. This support system will be there for you no matter what happens with your partner, and you will have to rely on someone. This strategy might relieve the burden and the pressure that is on your back.

The step you can make is to start making decisions on your own. There are those very important things that matter both to you and your partner, and these should be made together. However, if you are a codependent person, you will wait for your partner to decide on everything instead of you. If you gain control over at least the smallest things, it will be considered great progress.

Codependent persons are usually completely dependent on other people's will and decisions. Therefore, you need to start making small decisions and gradually move on to some bigger ones. So what if you make a mistake? Everyone else makes mistakes, learn from them, and move on. Even if you do make a wrong decision, usually there is enough time to fix it. Also, if you do not fix it, it will serve as a great lesson for the future. You will know that you need to consider some other things when decision making. These things will depend on what you are deciding on. However, leave those big decisions for together decision making. It is better to discuss the pros and cons of your partner than to make a huge mistake that a narcissist will most likely never forget. Thus, you should wait for you both to decide. However, there is one thing you should not do, and that is to let the narcissist decide for you.

Learn how to stabilize without anyone else's help. When you are codependent, it may seem like you have no idea how to calm down and look at things cool headedly. You need to try different techniques and find the one that works best for you. For example, you can listen to music, exercise, draw, and paint, play games, watch movies, whatever makes you think about something else, or whatever makes you express your feelings without ruining a relationship with someone you care about.

This can be a good tactic to keep you calm even if someone gets you angry or anxious. You just leave and do your thing to make you calm and happy again. It is much better than getting involved in an argument that might last forever if you are arguing with a narcissist.

Another thing that you have to have in mind is that you and your partner may not have the same opinions on all topics. And that is okay. There are no two persons that share the same opinions and views on everything. Diversity is good. If you live with a narcissist, they might try to make you think like them. They will insist on doing things their way.

You will need to be consistent and constantly say your opinion so that they understand that you have the right to have an opinion. On the other hand, if they do not have any interest in what you want to do, you can take one of your friends who enjoy such activities and go with them. It is just one more way to get closer to some of your friends and build your support group.

When it comes to goals, it is a great thing to have common goals with your partner. Those goals may not be the same as what you have set before your life with your partner.It will help you remember what your aims are. You may even change your mind about some goals over time, and that is okay.People change, so should their goals. If those goals do not match your partner's, you may get into a conflict.

However, you should compromise when those goals matter to both of you, and you should do it equally. If you are willing to give up on the part of your lifetime dream, then they should too. You should not allow a narcissist to control you so much that you do not even have dreams anymore. Having goals and dreams drives us forward, and no one should ever be able to ruin them. We must not allow anyone to do that. This is where setting boundaries comes in hand. You will tell them that you have other plans and that they do not coincide with theirs. You may compromise, but do strive to accomplish your biggest dreams.

The final step in getting more independence is to enjoy your life. It is too short to waste it on pleasing others who will probably not even notice the hard work you are putting in to please them. Therefore, enjoy each day, love yourself, and encourage yourself to win new battles each day.

Chapter 19. The Harm of Narcissistic Abuse

Narcissistic abuse can break down a person's self-esteem, eroding the very person they thought they knew. If you have suffered from narcissistic abuse, you may one day look in the mirror and not see someone you know. You may see someone, dead-eyed and resigned looking back at you, was once, and you saw someone filled with hope and joy.

The abuse endured from a narcissist can leave lasting damage, made worse when the victim struggles to escape, and it may escalate if the victim tries to escape. Amidst the emotional manipulation, the narcissist toys with the victim's mind in ways that most people would never even consider. The results can be a person with extensive damage to their emotional states and self-esteems that are long-lasting and difficult to heal without assistance.

Each of these effects is debilitating on their own. Still, when they all come together, the victim of narcissistic abuse is left reeling, mind racing in an attempt to make sense of the serious manipulation and distortion of reality that has occurred and feeling entirely off-balance. The results of narcissistic abuse create such characteristic results that it is often referred to as narcissistic abuse syndrome.

People who have suffered from narcissistic abuse frequently suffer from echoism and mental health issues resulting from long periods in which they were the victims.

Echoism

Have you heard the story of Narcissus and Echo? In this story, Narcissus was a handsome man who was hunting with a group in the forest. The nymph, Echo, sees Narcissus on his way through the forest and immediately falls in love. She had just been cursed to only repeat back what is said to her, so despite being quite enamored by Narcissus, she could not call out. When Narcissus eventually called out, and she answered, she was rejected by Narcissus. She was so heartbroken that she faded away, leaving behind only her voice to echo the sounds of other people.

The victim of narcissistic abuse becomes like Echo, fading away. Though the victim's physical body remains present, the personality and everything that made that individual unique and he or she fade away. Self-esteem falters, desires fade away, and the victim finds him- or herself entirely consumed with one purpose: Serving the narcissist at all costs.

When echoism occurs, you no longer feel like yourself. You feel as though you are stripped away from you, and you exist in the world rather than thriving. You are just as much a shadow, a voice on the wind, as Echo became when she allowed herself to love Narcissus. You are told that you are not good enough, that you will never be good enough, and you believe it.

Mental Health Issues

Along with echoism, suffering from narcissistic abuse also brings out mental health issues. People who have suffered from this abuse find their mental health strained due to always trying to survive. They are met continuously with cortisol, adrenaline, and norepinephrine, as they are perpetually living in stress. They are unable to truly relax, continually feeling as though they are attempting to make a life on thin ice that may shatter beneath them at any point in time—which they are.

The victim feels as though the only choice is catering to the narcissist's every whim to avoid an explosion.

Those who live with this kind of abuse tend to develop some of the significant mental health issues of anxiety, codependency, depression, and often also post-traumatic stress disorder.

People who lived through narcissistic abuse find themselves questioning whether they can perceive reality accurately. They think that their needs and wants are meaningless and must be sacrificed for the narcissist, and they frequently are very down on themselves. They do not see their value, instead of settling into a state of depression while always on edge about when the narcissist's abuse will strike next.

Thoughts of Suicide or Self-harming

All of those mental health issues come with an increased risk of self-harm and thoughts of suicide. Stressed and abused by the narcissist, afraid to breathe without permission, and feeling hopeless toward anything ever getting better, some victims of the narcissist will turn to thoughts of suicide or self-harm to cope. They may feel that death would be a release from the narcissist's abuse, and especially if they are feeling trapped with no escape, such as if they do not have a support network or access to the means to leave and may feel as they have no other choice.

Self-harm does not always look like cutting or physically leaving injuries, it can sometimes occur through self-medication and feeding addictions. The victim may turn to drugs or alcohol to cope with the narcissist's stress, frequently drinking too much or seeking out dangerous and addictive drugs. This sort of self-abuse can result in addiction, physical illness or injury, or even death. However, the release the victim feels in the moment feels worthwhile, and the victim risks serious addiction in the future to get that small, albeit dangerous, reprieve from the pain and numbness.

The Traits of Victims of Narcissistic Abuse

Narcissistic abuse victims typically present with a series of traits, not unlike that of the narcissist and the codependent. While sometimes the codependent and the abuse victim are the same, which is not always the case. Keep a general guide as to what to expect to see in situations of abuse, but do not treat it as a hard-and-fast rule.

Dissociation

Dissociation occurs when the victim starts to distance himself- or herself from any emotional states. It becomes easier to hide behind a veil of numbness than to face the abuse, and the victim retreats within him- or herself. This is a common sign seen in post-traumatic stress disorder or individuals who have suffered from some trauma. While this is beneficial when trying to survive some short-term or acute trauma, it is not a state that is healthy to live in long-term. No one is going to be happy or healthy living numbed and dissociated.

Distrustful

When always surrounded by abuse and manipulation, it becomes easy to grow distrustful. While you may continue to trust the narcissist, such as if he is gaslighting you and making you doubt yourself, you grow doubtful of your ability to understand the world around you and trust other people. If you do escape the narcissist, you are likely to have trouble believing other people or opening yourself up to future relationships. You may distrust anyone who dares to voice any concern about your situation, finding it more comfortable to live in denial than to confront the abuse head-on.

Fearful

Along with being distrustful, you may grow fearful as exposed to narcissistic abuse. The narcissist's explosive reactions and tendency to over-react has taught you to always be on edge, worrying about the narcissist's reaction, how other people may perceive his reactions, and what will happen to you. This fear leads to the constant production of stress hormones that keep you unable ever truly to relax.

Paranoid

Due to a combination of distrust and fearfulness, you may become paranoid. You think that you are untrustworthy, or unable to see situations. You become paranoid that you are being taken advantage of or trying to manipulate you, though this thought is typically directed toward everyone but the narcissist. The narcissist may be whispering in your ear that others are simply jealous of what the two of you share and that anyone who dares say anything against the narcissist only wants him for themselves.

Self-sacrificing

The narcissist wants his victims to surrender themselves fully to his whims, meeting his needs whenever necessary and forsaking their own. You often do this as a survival mechanism to satisfy the narcissist, but over time, you learn that your personal needs are unimportant. After extended periods of being unable to assert yourself or meet your own needs, you eventually forsake them all together, instead of finding purpose and temporary relief at meeting the narcissist needs as you recognize that a content narcissist is a narcissist that is not likely to lash out of you. Of course, that contentment is short-lived.

Blaming yourself

During this, you may blame yourself, feeling as though it is your fault. You may think that you could have been smarter or stronger to get away from the abuse before it escalated into something more. You may think that you have caused the abuse yourself, deserving of the abuse due to your incompetence or insufficiencies. You may feel that you, yourself, are just unworthy of love inherently. No matter the reason, you find yourself directing blame inwardly to make sense of the situation, although abuse is never the fault of the victim.

Self-sabotaging

Along with blaming yourself, you may get to the point of self-sabotage. Your self-esteem has been so damaged and twisted that you believe every word of what the narcissist says about your worth. You begin to act accordingly. If you are not good enough at cooking, for example, you may stop caring, thinking it does not matter anyway. This means that you may not pay attention to measurements because your food will come out poorly anyway. Because you never apply for jobs that allow you to live by yourself, you remain dependent on the narcissist.

Protecting their abuser

Perhaps the one nearly universal trait of abuse victims is the urge to protect the abuser vehemently. The victim is likely to protect the abuser, often still feeling loyal to the narcissist, or feeling in love with the person they thought the narcissist was. You may deny that the abuse was as bad as it may have been, or when someone tells you that the abuser is not a good person. You may point out all the ways you see the abuser as a good person, such as pointing to how he took you on a nice vacation and showers you with love when you are in the idealization stage in your relationship. This is enough for the victim, but it becomes clear to those around the victim that the relationship is not normal or healthy.

Chapter 20. Restoring Self-Esteem

The victims of narcissists are often chosen because they fit a particular character profile. It is important to revisit it here as it pinpoints those important aspects of raising self-esteem. Raising self-esteem is a critical part of the healing process, especially for codependent people who are at risk of falling prey to another narcissist after having left the first one.

The narcissist generally chooses people that are emotionally insecure, fragile, sensitive, empathic, and lacking in resilience. Individuals with these characteristics can be either women or men, and the narcissist knows just what signs to be on the lookout for to clue them in that you are this type of person.

What does this mean for you once you have decided to free yourself from the narcissist's control? It means that you need to work towards being less insecure, less fragile, and more resilient. Building self-esteem is the best way that you can improve in all of these areas.

Self-esteem is your internal sense of self-worth. The problem with many co-dependent or emotionally insecure people is that they allow others to determine their self-worth. This is generally not a state that they have for themselves to blame. It is very common in our society for men and women to look to others to validate them. If others do not like them or do not value them, they feel unhappy. Although some desire for social acceptance is normal, people who cannot function without it will be at higher risk for anxiety and depression, even leaving aside their predisposition towards codependent relationships.

The goal is not only to protect you from narcissists in the future but also to heal from the narcissistic abuse and earlier trauma. Although many steps can be undertaken to build up self-esteem, the following are areas of focus that are generally helpful:

- Acceptance
- Increase awareness
- Detach with love
- Changing reactions
- Being assertive
- Feed yourself
- Become autonomous and take control

Many people who become involved with narcissists are not able to accept aspects of them that they are not entirely comfortable. They look to others to give them the approval that they cannot give themselves. The problem is that the narcissist will never give you that sort of approval. You will have to accept yourself as you are which may involve what is called radical acceptance. Take a long, hard look in the mirror (the physical, external, and the internal mirror) and learn to accept and love yourself for who you are.

Loving yourself involves getting to know you better. Increase your awareness of yourself, which is a crucial step towards learning to accept and eventually love yourself. Once you have accomplished this, it will be easier for you to detach yourself from others in a more natural way as you no longer require them to fill a need that you have. Your reactions to the events around you will also change as your low self-esteem no longer causes you to personalize, magnify, and catastrophes' events.

Once you can approach interactions with self-esteem and a more normal sense of reality you will be able to assert yourself more. Individuals with low self-esteem have difficulty doing this, which is why building up your sense of self-worth is so important. Feed yourself by remembering those things that make you "you." You have value as a person, and you do not need another person to validate you. Once you understand this kind of self-sufficiency, you will be able to function as a healthy, autonomous person and take control of your life.

Good self-esteem does not significantly vary with events happening outside. When bad things happen to you, you won't feel bad about yourself because they are not reflections of your essential self. When codependents suffer low self-esteem, they suffer disappointment or loss. They also feel defeated.

Self-esteem has about two interrelated aspects;

- A sense of personal worth (respect to self) means an assurance of their value. It is an affirmative attitude towards one's right to live and be happy, having comfort in asserting thoughts, needs, and wants, making the joyful feeling your natural birthright.

- A sense of personal efficacy means confidence in the functioning of your mind, your ability to think for yourself, judge, decide, and choose. It is also the confidence to understand the facts of reality that are within your sphere of interest.

Both self-value and self-efficacy are the dual pillars of healthy self-esteem for every codependent individual. They are the significant characteristics of the term "self-esteem" because of their fundamentality. Self-efficacy generates a sense of control over the area of your life that is associated with the psychological wellbeing of an individual. Self-value makes a benevolent sense of community with other people, a fellowship of mutual regard, and independence.

How does a healthy self-esteem manifest?

There are simple and more direct ways in which healthy self-esteem manifests itself. They are as follows;

- A face or manner of talking and moving the pleasure of that project in being alive

- Comfort in giving and receiving compliments as an expression of appreciation and love

- Ability to preserve dignity under conditions of stress

- Flexibility in responding to challenges and situations

- Comfort with assertive behaviors in self and others

Conclusion

While you can do things to influence how the other parent thinks and behaves, you ultimately have no power to change a narcissist. The only thing you can truly control in your co-parenting situation is yourself. This can be a frustrating realization to come to Even if your co-parent is doing something wrong, or is bullheaded or annoying, you can do almost nothing to change it. So if you can't change that, it makes sense to focus on the things that are within your power to change. And it is unfair that just because the other parent can't pull it together that you should have to change what you're doing or how you are reacting, you're right to feel like that is ridiculous. But the reality is that if you want things to be different, you have to start with what you can control.

Accept reality. It can be quite annoying to realize that, for the most part, if you want to change, you have to make it happen. Work through your feelings about this entirely.

Know you're not wrong. In many situations, what you have been doing and how you have been reacting to your co-parent is not wrong. But there might be a different way of communicating, reacting, or responding that will achieve better results. What you've been doing isn't wrong, but there may be something else you could do that would work better in the situation.

Take things one day at a time. You can only deal with today right now, so don't try to think about anything else. If you've decided to change how you communicate, focus on improving the way you are communicating with the other parent today.

If your ex excludes you, you want to do the same thing to him. But the only way to break the cycle of problems with the other parent is to refuse to participate in the cycle.

Pause. Before you respond, take a breath. This allows you to react without a kneejerk reaction mindfully.

Step outside the conversation. Pretend you are someone watching the conversation. This will give you emotional distance and can help you decide what to say or do to defuse the problem. Look at what is happening with objectivity, and you can find the best way to react.

Think strategically. Instead of responding to your ex based on how you feel, try to respond in a manipulative way. Do or say what you need to do to get the response and actions you want. It's just better and more satisfying than speaking in anger or annoyance. It gets you to want and reduces the conflict all at the same time.

While you can never change the underlying problems between you and your ex, you can reduce their impact on your life. The more you see and talk to your ex, the greater the chance that there will be an argument or a disagreement or simply rubbing you the wrong way.

Make transfer times all business. You're there to exchange your child, not to talk. Do the transfer and get out.

Stay informed and nothing else. If you and your ex are keeping each other up to date on things like your child's schedule, health, grades, activities, and development, continue to do so, but keep things brief and to the point. Avoid lengthy conversations. Share relevant information and try to reduce the commentary. Don't stand around and talk about what a mutual friend is doing or what car you're considering buying.

Pull back. You don't have to answer every text, email, or phone call from your ex. You also don't have to respond to every comment, question, or barb. Deal with what has to be dealt with and decide not to get involved with anything else.

Maintain space. If you're both going to events for your child, that's a wonderful way to show your child you both are involved. You don't, however, have to sit together every time or any time. If you decide to share birthdays and holidays, there are ways to both participate in the party or celebration without having to have a lot of in-depth, direct interaction with each other. Stay focused on your child. Avoid side comments to each other. Even avoiding eye contact can help you maintain distance.

Take it slowly. If one day you are talking, emailing, and texting with your ex all the time and the following day you're suddenly unresponsive, this is likely going to create a whole other set of problems. Try to gradually reduce your contact for a couple of weeks, so it does not feel as if you are freezing your ex-out from anger.

Often in situations with your ex, you may feel as it is a "me vs. you" situation. Every decision or choice seems to come down to one person winning and the other person losing. This can lead to ongoing negative feelings about all contact with your ex and can leave you constantly on the defensive. It's possible to reframe these situations, so you're not thinking about whether you or your ex benefit, but whether your child benefits.

Less conflict benefits your child. Children exposed to a lot of conflict experience stress, anxiety, and worry. Making choices that minimize conflict is something that directly benefits your child.

Use the best interests as your compass. When the court makes custody decisions, it does so based on what is in your child's best interests. This is a useful way to make decisions yourself. When you're thinking about what to do or say, ask yourself what would be best for your child. Shifting the question from what you want or what you think would best to what is best for your child can clarify a lot of issues. You might not want your child to spend your ex's birthday with him, but doing so would probably make your child happy. Take yourself out of the equation.

In the first few years after a divorce or separation, parenting is a challenge. There is so much to work out and so many feelings that remain raw. Everything is new, and nothing is as it was. But if you talk to friends who have been through a divorce, they will tell you that things gradually settle down. You eventually get into a routine with the other parent, and although there may be bumps in the road, in general, things tend to even out.

Keep your perspective. The issues and concerns you are having with your ex today will not be the same in two years. Problems will resolve, and the things that felt insurmountable and impossible will be in your rearview mirror. While it's essential to pay attention to what is happening today, it's also a good idea to keep some perspective and remember that things will improve.

Know that everything will change. Your child is not static, so he is going to grow and develop, and his needs will be drastically different in a few years. Most parents find they need to adjust their parenting plan as they go, taking into account their children's sports, activities, hobbies, friends, and eventually, jobs. Because of this, even if your current situation is not exactly as you would like it, it's all going to have to change eventually anyhow.

Co-parenting is one of the bravest and hardest things you will ever do in your life. More than anything give yourself credit for the hard work and remember that your child will never forget the love you've shown.

Made in the USA
Monee, IL
21 November 2020

48889420R00090